THE DAY WAS MADE FOR WALKING

An Aussie's Search for Meaning on the Camino de Santiago

NOEL BRAUN

ABOUT THE AUTHOR

Noel Braun commenced his working career as a country school teacher, then moved into a corporate career, which took him from Melbourne to Perth and Sydney. He has had a lifelong passion for writing and wrote the first words of his novels nearly forty years ago. After a busy career and raising a family of four, he has found the time in retirement to fulfil his long-held ambition and see his work in print.

Noel has published two novels: *Friend and Philosopher* and *Whistler Street*. He has also published a memoir, *No Way to Behave at a Funeral*, which describes his journey following the death by suicide of his wife Maris. He is working on other manuscripts and on developing a new career in writing.

Noel lives on Sydney's northern beaches. He is a keen walker and enjoys getting out in the national parks surrounding his home.

Published in Australia by Sid Harta Publishers Pty Ltd,
ABN: 46 119 415 842
23 Stirling Crescent, Glen Waverley, Victoria
3150 Australia
Telephone: +61 3 9560 9920, Facsimile: +61 3 9545 1742
E-mail: author@sidharta.com.au

First published in Australia 2013
This edition published 2017
Copyright © Noel Braun 2013
Cover design, typesetting: Chameleon Print Design

The right of Noel Braun to be identified as the Author of the Work has been asserted in accordance with the Copyright, Designs and Patents Act 1988.

Braun, Noel
The Day Was Made for Walking
ISBN: 1-922086-47-9
EAN13: 978-1-922086-47-1
pp270

Dedicated to the memory of my cherished wife, Maris,
whose support, confidence and quiet encouragement
inspired me, and continues to do so

We are pilgrims on the journey
We are brothers on the road
We are here to help each other
Walk the mile and bear the load.

– From 'The Servant Song' by Richard Gillard.

CONTENTS

Act Two – Spain
El Camino de Santiago de Compostela

Prologue

The Way of St James

1. A journey of the heart and soul

I was shit-scared. My heart was pounding. My guts ached. I could smell my own sweat.

I was in legendary Le Puy-en-Velay in the Haute Loire France and stood in the porch of the cathedral Notre Dame de Puy, striking in its dominance. I looked past the ancient town below, beyond the modern city to the surrounding mountain ridges and imagined over the horizon that Santiago and Saint James were beckoning.

I glanced down the long daunting flight of steps. I could think of no valid reason to delay, so, before I lost my nerve, I took my first wobbly step into the unknown. I'd received my pilgrim's blessing at the Pilgrims' Mass where I prayed for St James' protection.

With pack on my back, and pilgrim shell attached, I walked down the narrow street. A plaque announced that I was passing the spot where was born the Via Podiensis, the great route of pilgrimage towards Santiago de Compostela. A signpost indicated 1521 kilometres to go.

Only 1521 kilometres!

The day was Monday, 15 August 2010.

I was about to set out on *the Way of Saint James*, or in Spanish *El Camino de Santiago de Compostela*, or in French *Le Chemin de Saint-Jacques de Compostelle*. It's a long distance footpath with a difference. People have been walking it as a pilgrimage route for over a thousand years. I imagine that the 1500 kilometres route from Le Puy-en-Velay in the Haute Loire, France, to

Santiago – the supposed burial place of Saint James the Apostle, in the western part of Galicia, Spain – has changed little in that time. Parts of it are now modern tarred roads, and many of the hospitals and other accommodation set up by religious orders along the way to cater for the needs of pilgrims have long disappeared. The practice of pilgrimage has been resurrected in modern times and today's pilgrims still follow the path taken by the medieval pilgrims; a route that passes through the same villages, climbs the same hills, crosses the same rivers and passes the same churches, chapels and cathedrals.

The earliest records of visits to the shrine dedicated to St James at Santiago de Compostela date from the 8th century. By the early 12th century the pilgrimage had become a highly organised business and brought together people from all over Europe from all classes and stations. The daily needs of pilgrims on their way to and from Santiago were met by a series of hospitals and hospices. These had royal protection. The whole pilgrimage route was possible because of the protection provided by the kingdom of France. Pilgrims walked, often for months, to arrive at the great church in Santiago de Compostela to pay homage to St James. Over time the pilgrimage to the shrine became the most renowned medieval pilgrimage, the other main pilgrimages being to Rome and Jerusalem.

It was a custom for those medieval pilgrims to take home a scallop shell picked up on the Galician beaches as proof of their journey's completion. Gradually, the shell became the Christian symbol for St James. Many pilgrims wore one as a sign that they were pilgrims. To wear the shell was to hold a position of protected reverence. It gave them privileges; to sleep in churches and to ask for meals. It helped to ward off thieves. The Church excommunicated anyone who attacked them.

Over the centuries many myths evolved about the shell. One

of these concerns the body of St James, which was lost overboard in a storm on his boat trip to Galicia. However, the body was washed ashore undamaged and covered in shells. The shell was also a metaphor for the pilgrim. As the waves of the ocean wash scallop shells up on the shore, God's hand also guides the pilgrims to Santiago.

The word *Compostela* itself means 'field of stars'. According to one medieval legend the Milky Way was formed by the dust raised by travelling pilgrims. Another version relates how St James appeared in a dream to Charlemagne, urging him to liberate his tomb from the Moors, who occupied Spain at the time, and showing him the direction to follow by the route of the Milky Way.

Today, there seems to be just as many pilgrims on the road as in medieval times. Tens of thousands of them and other travellers as well make their way to Santiago de Compostela, by foot or by bicycle. Some travel the whole distance in one go. Others cover it in sections and take years. For some it's a long-distance walk; for others it's a holiday, a rest from the stresses of their daily lives. Others are there for the adventure of travelling through a foreign country.

Others are wrapped in the historical and cultural context. The Camino has left behind a legacy of medieval Christianity, with its countless religious icons, churches and reminders of what the church and other authorities established for the welfare of the passing pilgrims. It's like walking through an open door museum. The route has become so revered that it was declared the first European Cultural Route by the Council of Europe in 1987; it was also named one of UNESCO's World Heritage Sites.

Others' motivations are spiritual. They remove themselves from the everyday bustle and, in the solitude of long distance

walking, seek meaning. They are facing a transition or a significant event in their lives such as retirement or bereavement. They are processing a major crisis in their lives. They are longing for healing or resolution. Others want time out to review their lives and set a new direction. They are running from failure and looking for enlightenment. They are seeking a challenge that will push them, inspire them and save them.

A few have religious yearnings. They may feel that their faith has grown stale, or have a desire for intense prayer or want to explore and better understand their beliefs. They may wish to atone for past sins. Enduring deprivation and hardship is an important aspect of the experience. The external physical journey is a metaphor for a journey of the soul.

For the medieval pilgrim, the pilgrimage was not just the physical arrival at a holy place but the experience of progress towards that destination. The experience was just as important as the holy place itself. Similarly, for the modern pilgrim with spiritual or religious motivation, the pilgrimage is an intensely internal experience in an intensely physical context in which the journey itself, more than the destination, is the goal.

I had heard of the Camino but it was never more than a distant thought, like far away rumbling over the horizon. I never imagined I would walk it until one day ...

2. In the silence and solitude, I might feel closer to God

I n 1999 I read in our parish magazine an account of the Camino. My fellow parishioner and friend, Mike Fuller-Lewis, undertook the pilgrimage with his daughter. His experience enthralled me. If he could do it, why couldn't I? My beloved wife Maris was passionate about travel, but the Camino did not impress her. Instead we visited Ireland and Japan, toured the UK by car and embarked on a pilgrimage through Turkey, Greece and Italy. Things changed. For many years Maris struggled with depression, at first for a few weeks each year. She found relief in our travel, but the affliction engulfed her and poisoned every moment of her life until travel was out of the question. Her depression worsened and she succumbed to suicide in October 2004.

Her death was catastrophic, like a massive flood that changed the course of my life forever. Overwhelmed with pain and guilt I was swept to a place so remote that I felt close to madness. I was on the brink of despair. When the experts say that persons bereaved by suicide are themselves at risk, I knew exactly what they were driving at. Somehow I had to find my way out of the morass.

Travel might keep me busy and help my grieving, I thought.

I travelled to America and Europe early 2005 just a few months after her death. That was a bad, bad mistake, a mere diversionary tactic because the pain of loss was still just as intense. My grief was waiting when I returned home, lurking in the corridors and rooms like a snarling demon, ready to pounce and engulf me.

As life became less insane I travelled in 2006 to France. I lived in Chambéry for three months. At the cathedral I heard the bishop urging the young people to undertake a pilgrimage to Santiago. Then I witnessed the farewell of a group complete with backpacks and shells.

I knew the Camino had to be my next project.

All the while, I was processing Maris' death. My retirement could have been a dismal wasteland but I adjusted to her absence and led a normal life – a different kind of normal, mind you, to the life I had with her. She left a hollow. I had to find some meaning for my suffering, to even use it for good, otherwise I'd close up and close down. I wrote about my grief. As well as therapy for me, I hoped my story might help others who were on the same journey. I threw myself into my voluntary work with Lifeline and became involved in facilitating suicide bereavement support groups where people who have lost a loved one to suicide are able to find support from one another. Somehow I was brought to life again and gradually I put the pieces together.

Each year, I considered I should go on the Camino that year, but each year came and went.

At the same time, my brother-in-law, Joe, was sick. He suffered from cancer and also had heart problems. With each low point we braced ourselves for a possible end. I put off travelling in 2009 in case Joe died while I was away. I travelled to Queensland to join my sister Maria in celebrating his 80th birthday. He was in hospital and as his family stood around his bed singing 'Happy Birthday' I wondered how long he would be with us because he looked so shrunken and fragile in his neat white bed festooned with balloons, birthday and get-well

2. In the silence and solitude, I might feel closer to God

cards. He left hospital soon after. I thought it was a good sign. It did not dawn on me that perhaps he was sent home because the medicos decided they could do no more for him. Early in 2010 he seemed to stabilise. He was getting no better but he wasn't getting worse.

I talked to my children. I have four – two girls and two boys: Angela, the eldest, then Stephen, Jacinta and Tim. They have been wonderfully supportive since their mother's death. In fact, Angela once said, 'Dad, you're our only parent now. We've got to look after you.' At the same time, they had been encouraging me to do what I wanted, pleased to see that I had not collapsed in a heap (to use one of Maris' terms) but had been leading a full albeit restless life.

The four had the same response to my question: 'Dad, go for it.'

I booked my flight to Paris. I was committed.

I visited Joe and Maria in Queensland in the week before I left and found Joe in good spirits.

'I'm taking a punt, Joe, that you'll be around when I return,' I confided to him.

'I won't fall off the perch while you're away,' were his last words to me. I had the guilts about leaving him but I had to go.

I couldn't wait any longer. The Camino was dragging me like a magnet, an urgent challenge, pressing an invitation I could not refuse. I could not have accepted earlier because I had heart problems. In 2007 I developed chest pains. I had an angiogram and a stent inserted in one of the major arteries. My cardiologist suggested I may have had an earlier heart attack and my heart had repaired itself. That didn't surprise me as I remember clearly the broken heart feeling after Maris' death. But in 2010, I had a healthy body. In my late seventies, I was retired and without the snare of ambition or the encumbrance of a job. I was free of the rigours and restrictions of rearing a family.

Many of my friends found it difficult to understand why I'd want to do the Camino. All they could see was my age and what a long and arduous a journey it would be – not their idea of a holiday. I found it hard to convince them that I wasn't going on a holiday. I was not a tourist. I wasn't going to France and Spain to gawk at museums and medieval churches. I was a pilgrim. The Camino would take me into the territory of the heart and the soul. Six years after my wife's death I was trying to find myself. Who was I without Maris? Her death made a mockery of all my assumptions about the remainder of my life.

How do you make God laugh? was a joke that resonated with me.

Answer: *Make plans for the future.*

It was a time of questions I thought I had answered years ago. At the age of seventy-seven I was asking myself, *Who the hell am I?* I was a restless vagabond drifting in search of a stable anchorage. Would the Camino give me a concrete structure? Would the Camino be my teacher and show me the way? They were the questions that hammered at my heart.

I have bushwalked for much of my life and I valued the opportunity for extensive physical exertion. But I hoped the Camino was more than a physical challenge. I was embarking on an inner spiritual journey that was uniquely mine. Spirituality is different for everyone. Strongest in my thinking was the idea of a journey of self-discovery, of learning who I was and wanted to be. There was also the challenge of reaching beyond my current limits. This applied not only to physical challenges but also to stepping beyond my comfort zones, keeping an open mind, and questioning beliefs that I may have held most of my life.

While spirituality is personal, it's also rooted in being connected with others and with the surrounding world. At the same time it's connected to an acknowledgement of a higher power, something that is bigger and beyond you, whether rooted in a belief in God, or in nature or some unknown essence.

Was I up to the task? It's one thing to walk 15–20 kilometres in a day, but to push on day after day required fitness and courage. Would my old body and spirit cope with the physical and emotional pounding? I like to believe that I have a tenacity that does not recoil from what is hard to do.

I couldn't just turn up in France and start walking. I packed heaps into my preparation, far more than if I were a younger man. I worked on my fitness. I regard my body as a gift that has to be cared for, so I've always been a gym junkie. I told my personal trainer, Jenni, what I was on about and she worked me hard, as if she were preparing an old stallion for a tough race. I walked the local streets and the adjacent National Park with full backpack.

A curious neighbour leaned over his fence. 'What are you in training for?' he asked. 'It must be some kind of trek.'

I took care with my boots. I bought them about a year previously. I take size forty-four, but the salesman at one of Sydney's leading outdoor shops recommended size forty-three. 'They'll be a tight fit, but your feet won't move and the chances of blisters by rubbing minimised.' With misgivings I accepted his advice and bought a top-of-the range brand. After wearing them for a while, I had the local boot maker stretch them, so that the fit was snug but perfect.

I spent the last night with my daughter Angela. As well as giving up her bed for me, my granddaughter Eliza 'loaned' me her Aussie cap and flag. As I tossed in the narrow bed and tried to sleep, my mind was far too active. I was frantic. What on Earth was I taking on? I had visions of catastrophe, of collapsing with exhaustion and breaking a leg.

'I should take the easy path,' I said to myself. 'The Camino's too much for a seventy-seven-year-old.'

I prayed that I would meet my challenges with Cs rather than Ss. I developed my Cs and Ss formula shortly after Maris' death, as a resolution for my new life without her.

Meet my challenges with Cs rather than Ss. C stands for Confidence, Courage, Conviction, Curiosity and Compassion. S stands for Safety, Security or Social Approval. I should always be ready to challenge myself, to step beyond the boundaries. I should not be too concerned about safe options, security or what people might think of my actions.

I'm as prepared as I'll ever be, I prayed. Okay, God, it's in your hands now.

Act One

France
Le Chemin de Saint-Jacques-de-Compostelle

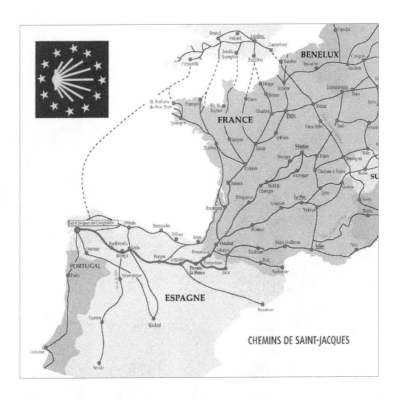

CHEMINS DE SAINT-JACQUES

3. Walk within you. Listen to my footfalls in your heart

At the airport check-in the lady gave me a second look as I placed my backpack rather self-consciously on the scales. Was she thinking, *What's this old chap doing with a backpack?* It weighed eighteen kilograms. That was ridiculous! Far too heavy! I was alarmed. I would have to get rid of several kilograms before I could begin walking.

As I went through Customs and Immigration – confronting at the best of times – my heart was pounding and my stomach ached. My mouth was dry. I'd been plucked out of a safe, secure and comfortable environment to face the unknown. I craved reassurance so I reached for the familiar cross around my neck which I've worn since Maris' death. Our daughter Angela gave it to her after a trip to Ireland. Maris had worn it since. They'd removed it from her broken body in the hospital where she was declared dead, given it to me and now I wear it.

My thoughts turned to a small wooden cross secure in my backpack. It was made of driftwood, which I picked up on a beach in Oregon one time I was having a bad day. I regard it as a link with eternity. How long was the driftwood on the beach? What was the age of the original tree? Whenever I travel I take that cross with me. Both crosses are always with me. I prayed that I would have a safe journey. I wished Maris was with me, but I knew she was in spirit. I had dedicated my walk to her memory. I was taking her in my heart every exhilarating and fearsome step of the way.

By the time the plane reached New Guinea I had settled

down, more or less used to the idea that I was underway. As we passed over Japan, I followed the flight map and noted cities such as Kumamoto and Fukuoku, which Maris and I visited on our first overseas trip together. I had a stopover in Seoul. Like the pilgrims of old I had to pass through many countries to get to my destination. They left their homelands to plod over mountains and plains, along a path of their dreams through dangerous times when many barely survived and others never returned home.

At Charles de Galle Airport, I passed through immigration without any hassles, but buying a ticket for the train to Paris took patience. As a pilgrim in a foreign land I was determined to use public transport. All the trains were late as there had been a strike that afternoon, but once I was on Métro Line 1 I found Port de Vincennes without any problems.

Finding the hostel *Centre International de Séjour Maurice Ravel* was another challenge. Four hours after the plane landed I lay on a bed in the tiniest of rooms on the sixth floor, which took as much trouble to find as the hostel.

I was exhausted but I had made it.

After four years I felt happy to be back in France. I was a wanderer, a pilgrim and a vagabond again. I was in this pilgrimage business up to my neck, thankful that I had the health and fitness for such a caper. I needed a beer. I didn't recall passing a bar on the way from the metro and the thought of going out to find one was too daunting, so I rolled over and went to sleep.

I had one day in Paris. I had explored the city on earlier visits and knew that the term 'the city of light' is well deserved, but this time I was not a tourist. I was passing through to complete a quest. The city was overrun with visitors and I avoided Notre Dame Cathedral where the queues ran across the square but I crossed the Seine and found rue Saint Jacques and the church of Saint Jacques. In contrast to the busy streets the interior was tranquil. No tourist throngs!

In a quiet corner I found a shrine to Saint Jacques, a wooden statue and below a pilgrim's blessing:

We humbly ask your blessing.

I lit a candle, watched the flickering flame and prayed for a good pilgrimage. I felt calm, at peace and ready. I sensed that the centuries were merging and that I was moving into another world. I thought of thousands before me who had paused before an image of Saint James.

Next day I took the metro to Chatelet to visit *La Tour de Saint Jacques* (Saint James' tower), the starting point for the medieval pilgrims and also for those modern pilgrims who walk to Santiago from Paris. I found the tower in the centre of a small park where a screen of hedges and trees created a delightful refuge from the bustle of the surrounding streets. I paused before a plaque commemorating the pilgrims of old. Despite the din of traffic penetrating the screen I felt a moment of peace, connection and readiness. I had commenced my pilgrimage.

I took the metro to Gare de Lyon and crossed the Seine to Gare Austerlitz for the train to Amboise in the Loire Valley. I had arranged to spend three weeks at a French language school brushing up my skills.

Anxieties crowded in. What would my host family be like? When I studied French at Chambéry in 2006 I lived in my own apartment, but this time I would be living with a family, part of the total immersion experience (*immersion totale*) where I would eat, drink, shower, shit and sleep. I was venturing into unknown fields. I reminded myself of my Cs and Ss. Meet my challenges with courage, confidence and conviction.

I had absolutely nothing to worry about. My hosts met me at the station. I spotted them as I stepped off the train. What a charming couple! Their faces beamed with smiles as they walked towards me.

Danièle and Michelle took me to their home, a pleasant suburban house in a new estate on a hill overlooking the town. We spent the afternoon chatting over coffee and cakes. They had no English so conversation was in French. Out of the recesses of my mind I dug deeply to remember vocabulary and grammar. Danièle was a retired chef and Michelle a retired nurse. In their retirement they looked after foreign students. I was to find that Danièle had lost none of his skills for he cooked excellent meals with a careful attention to presentation.

They had two other students. Maya was a Japanese girl about twenty-two and Marie was Columbian aged sixteen. I met Maya, a very sweet, gracious girl. Over a beautiful chicken and salad dinner we discussed family. Danièle and Michelle had one son whose job had taken him to Slovenia. He rang every Sunday night. Maya's family lived in Japan but were regular visitors to France. They were keen to know more of me and my family. I told them about my four children and six grandchildren. I mentioned my sister Maria and her sick husband Joe.

Monday morning over breakfast I met Marie who had gone to Paris for the weekend. In contrast to Maya's quiet and gentle nature, Marie was brassy, exuberant and loud. Michele was worried that I would get lost on the way to school and wrote down detailed instructions but Maya took upon herself the job of guide and walked with me. I went through the enrolment administration and a test to determine my level of French. All the students assembled at a morning coffee break and the principal welcomed the new students. In all, there were forty students assigned to four classes.

The principal was proud of her establishment and ran through the nationalities present – German, Swiss, Brazilian, Spanish, Columbian, American, and Japanese. I was the only Australian. The majority of the students were in their late teens or early twenties. I was the eldest by far, the granddaddy.

Tuesday saw my first full morning of classes. Marie and Maya walked to school with me – a quaint trio. We walked all the way downhill, passing from the new estate with its wide streets and modern cream-painted houses with gardens to the old town with its ancient buildings and crooked narrow lanes.

The girls were curious. Why was I studying French? I told them I had studied French for three months at Chambéry in 2006 and decided I needed a refresher in preparation for the Camino. That made them curious about the Camino and pilgrimages.

No time for further questions as we arrived at the school, an old delightfully decayed two story building with a clock in the tower that didn't work and a large front door that, when slammed shut by the wind, had the whole building in shock.

There I renewed my love affair with the seductive French tongue, the language of Molière, Honoré de Balzac, Emile Zola, Alexandre Dumas, Victor Hugo and many other greats. Not that I wished to study these classics. I was more concerned with the language of everyday people. It was a troubled romance as the French language can be a capricious lover. Just as you think you are getting intimate, she keeps her distance and makes you aware how little you know her.

In the afternoon I went shopping. Amboise's narrow ancient streets overflowed with shops catering for the multitude of tourists who, after visiting the chateau overlooking the town, spent their day eating a long lunch in the street cafes or ambling from shop to shop in search of souvenirs.

Each day I passed by an historic church, Saint Denis, dating from the 12th century, so I left the bright day outside and entered the ancient dim interior and lit a candle for Maris.

At home, Michele asked questions about my wife. She had seen the photo of Maris which I carried with me and placed on the bedside table. I spoke about Maris' depression and suicide, which I must admit saddened me in the telling. I tried to hold back a tear but I'm afraid it escaped. I made a mess of hiding it from Michele. I felt vulnerable as if I was baring my soul.

In the evening Danièle prepared another gourmet meal – escalope pork followed by chocolate mousse – so beautifully presented that I had to take a photo. I had struck it sweet with my family. It was delightful how Danièle and Michele were prepared to linger over the meal for up to two hours engaged in conversation. They were a wonderful example of how the French take their eating seriously. They refused to rush and savoured every mouthful. Dinner was a lesson in French. They listened patiently to the three of us explaining ourselves, their eyes lighting up when they got the point and correcting us if necessary. They were excellent teachers. I learned as much over their dinner table as in class.

On Wednesday morning I woke from a vivid dream in which Maris had returned. I said to her, 'I hope you're real and not just a dream.' I was bitterly disappointed.

My head was full of negativity. I have learned from years of practice to dismiss my early morning thoughts. As I cross the border into consciousness, I often find myself in a raw and desperate place. I am struck by pre-dawn anxiety. I carry on a debate with myself and try to sort out my mind, looking objectively at my situation. I entertained backing out, not only of the French school but the Camino as well. I swore at myself. What a bloody dill I am! Haven't I had these early morning terrors since I was a kid, recalling that there was usually nothing to worry about, and when there was, I always handled it?

On the walk to school, the girls asked a lot of questions about Maris. Michele had told them my story. Would I marry again? I admired their uncomplicated candour. It's a simple question but it touches a depth of emotion. Am I ready to move on? Do I really want to move on? Try explaining such feelings in a foreign language to two young girls on the cusp of life with their romantic ideas about love. I told them about the matchmaking efforts of some of my friends, which prompted a few giggles and quite a discussion, the 'wise' Marie explaining the concept to Maya. I said that perhaps I was a one-woman man. They found that romantic.

After class, I had lunch with the girls in the sunny courtyard and they were keen to pursue the morning's topic. Maya wanted to know how I met Maris, so I told them the story of meeting her at a dance. I saw this attractive girl knocking back all the boys, so I tried my luck and she accepted. That really set the girls off. I managed to extract myself to send an email to the family and was pleased to read theirs.

On the way home I visited the church of St Denis to find my candle still burning. Next to the candles was a book of prayers and petitions. I read an entry from a lady by name Audrey.

Seigneur, je suis tellement malheureuse. Aidez-moi à me sortir de cette dépression et de trouver enfin la Bonheur dans l'avenir. Merci, Audrey.

(Lord, I'm so miserable. Help me to pull through this depression and to find happiness at last in the future.)

My heart went out to Audrey. I thought of my Maris and her struggles. She was constantly searching for relief and tried everything – self-help books, meditation, hypnotherapy, medication and fish oil. She finally found the solution in death. I wrote a prayer for Audrey that her relief was not far away, that she would not arrive at the same solution as Maris.

The week settled into a routine. Breakfast consisted of bread and jam. I never got used to the French breakfast. They devote all their gastronomic energies to lunch and dinner, and neglect their *petit dejeuner*. Then we walked to school, about twenty-five minutes, ample time for chatting. After morning classes, we had lunch in the town or back at the school. The choice of food was limitless. You could select one of the many street cafes and eat a meal costing twenty euros (or more with wine). We students left the restaurants to the tourists and visited the *boulangeries* (bakers) instead and bought ourselves a baguette for less than a euro.

Sometimes we bought the fillings such as *jambon* (ham) or *fromage* (cheese) and made ourselves sandwiches, and sometimes the *boulanger* made the sandwiches for us for three or four euros. We'd sit in the sun back at the school, along the river or by the rampart wall of the chateau. The afternoons were passed in either shopping or exploring a little more of the town. Sometimes, I crossed the bridge, explored the river banks and looked back in awe at the chateau dominating the town. One afternoon, I visited the chateau, once the home of the kings of France. Standing on the parapet you could look down on the town with its maze of streets and laneways, filled with street cafes and tourists. Your gaze wandered to the river Loire, a broad expanse of water complete with bridge, small islands, mini-rapids, and fishermen, trying their luck from the banks or small boats. You looked up the hill covered with

modern houses and to the surrounding countryside of the
Loire valley, replete with its many chateaux. The views were
awesome.

On my walk home, I would visit Saint Denis and light
another candle. At home, some time for study or homework
would precede dinner at 7.00 pm. The meal and conversation
would stretch well into the evening. I would often go for a walk
after dinner in the long twilight and when I returned I could
hear Marie in the adjacent room talking in Spanish by Skype
to her mother in Columbia.

Each Friday a number of students departed and the principal gave a short message of thanks and goodbye at the morning
break. A young Brazilian student, a big handsome fellow, who
was leaving that day spoke to me in English. He gave a speech
in which he expressed admiration and respect for my enroll-
ing at the school at my age. He hoped that he could be like me
when he was my age. His words surprised me for we hadn't
spoken to each other before. I like to think that I'm an ordinary
bloke who doesn't take himself too seriously, who has given up
pretence or trying to make a good impression.

On Monday evening I returned to my room after dinner and
I noticed I had received a call. It was from my sister Maria. I
checked the time and realised, taking into account the time
difference between France and Queensland, it was about 4.00
am. There was only one reason she would call at that time.
I could feel the panic rising and my heartbeat quicken as I
returned her call, hoping she'd mucked up the time difference.
No greeting, she came straight to the point.

'Joe died.'

Maria blurted out the details. Joe complained he felt unwell
and without warning collapsed on the bedroom floor and died.
She could not raise her neighbours but rang a friend, Frank,

a short distance away and he came promptly. I felt guilty. I had left Maria in the lurch. I should be in Australia. I should be with my sister, comforting and supporting her, not on the other side of the world. I felt a real bastard. I tried to console her as she repeated the story. I hung up. I felt confused, weak and vulnerable. I had to talk to someone so I went downstairs and found Danièle and Michele watching TV. I was shaking. They were very caring. Michele gave me a hug. I returned upstairs wondering what I should do. I rang Maria and said I would return home to be with her. She seemed surprised and said she did not expect me to. I did not sleep that night. In the morning Marie and Maya were very supportive. Michele had told them the news. I didn't concentrate well on my lessons that morning. During the day I spoke to Angela and Jacinta. They both told me no one wanted me to come home. All the four children were planning to go to the funeral in Beenleigh, Queensland: Angela and Jacinta from Sydney, Tim from Melbourne and Stephen from Tamworth. My relief was immense. My children loved their Uncle Joe. Stephen rang. He agreed with the girls and told me to stay in France and continue my pilgrimage. Auntie Rea would need me when I came home in about ten weeks. Jacinta rang again. She was strapped for cash and Tim had offered to pay her air fare. I felt proud of my children. They loved their auntie Ree, as they called Maria, and were rallying around her in her time of need. My sister Maria had spent a lot of time with the children when they were younger. She had cared for them when Maris was sick and now they were putting their own convenience aside and coming to her support. They would do a more than adequate job of representing me.

I visited St Denis and lit two candles. I had planned to light a candle for Maris in every church I passed, but now I would light one for Joe. Lighting candles for deceased loved ones is an old tradition. A candle means more. It's a symbol. It speaks of light, hope, warmth and love. In burning itself out, it gives light and life to others. A lighted candle prolongs my prayer. It burns after I have left the church. The candle of hope is never extinguished.

I was in touch with the family many times. Maria and her daughter Anne were working on accommodation for all the family. Maria and Joe lived in a retirement village and so friends in the village were a possibility. In the phone calls I received news of the arrangements people were making to get to Queensland. In the meantime, life continued at Amboise. Other students spoke to me. Marie and Maya had told them my story and soon I was part of the school gossip. Noel the old Australian was grieving over the suicide of his wife and now his brother-in-law had died. I felt humbled by the care and compassion of these young people.

Sunday was a quiet day. I attended Mass at Saint Denis. I had noticed the young couple in the seat in front of me. She was beautiful in her slim fitting dress. At the Sign of Peace he leant across and kissed her tenderly. That sign of affection sent me to another world of the many times I kissed Maris gently and lovingly and I felt an intense sense of loss, on my own in Amboise, on the other side of the world while the family was gathering in Queensland. I found myself taunted by echoes of home – the kookaburras laughing in my pre-dawn garden, the morning sun streaming across my bed, my cat meowing for her breakfast.

Monday was the day of Joe's funeral but by the time I woke in France, it was over. Phone calls and emails from the family told me the story. The day went well was the consensus. Joe's son-in-law John read the eulogy which was sad, witty and, according to my brother Tom, reminded them that Joe would be missed both by his family and for his contribution to the retirement village life. The family read the prayers and readings. His grandson Michael read the reflection poem 'Walk within you', but lost the plot and wept with the final lines: *Be still, Close your eyes. Breathe; Listen to my footfall in your heart.* It sounded heartbreaking. All the family mentioned Abigail my granddaughter, aged three, who in her delightful innocence waved at the hearse saying, 'Bye bye.' She was intuitive to the occasion. My brother added in his email:

> I feel Ange, Cint, Tim and Stephen found the funeral difficult as it reminded them of Maris' sad passing. Noel, I'm so glad the kids forbade your premature return as you will have the opportunity to comfort Maria later on when she may possibly need it more, trying to get her life back to normal ... I hope I have been able to convey the sadness, the high regard held for Joe and the degree of comfort given to Maria.

It's impossible to underestimate the importance of a funeral, a place of public ritual. Family and friends were present, prepared to immerse themselves in the rituals of mourning. Maria did not have to face her loss alone. Joe had selected the songs and prayers. The family had the opportunity to tell his story, express their love and acknowledge his contribution to the family and the world. Life's journey is a pilgrimage and Joe had completed his.

Back in Amboise there were only a few days left. The task ahead loomed. Learning French was a pilgrimage in itself but I had come to France not to learn French but to walk the Camino. My worries returned. Was I up to the challenge?

Endless self-doubt nagged me, but something was dragging me forward. I had dedicated the Camino to Maris' memory, but my motivation was more, like a yearning of the spirit. A deep inner urge was driving me to endure the hardships and uncertainties of many weeks on the road.

I bought gifts for the family and needed three post office boxes to send them back to Australia. I lightened my backpack by sorting its contents into essentials and despatched the surplus with the gifts. The penultimate night, I dreamed of Maris. I was overjoyed to see her and gave her a hug. She collapsed as if she were only a shadow. Was her spirit visiting to wish me well on the Camino? On the last day I received my certificate and said my goodbyes. I was both happy and sad to leave. I lit my last candles at Saint Denis.

The final evening was extraordinary. I gave Michele and Danièle a book about Sydney as well as the cap and flag that Eliza had lent me. Danièle gave me a scallop shell, the symbol of the Camino and the mark of the pilgrim. The same shell that had watched over thousands of others would watch over me as I bowed my head to the path and cast my eyes down in search of signs that would keep me pointed towards Santiago.

I was astounded when Maya gave me a beautifully prepared album of photos taken during the three weeks along with a commentary in perfect French. Michele had me write in a book which contained an entry from all the previous students. I was the fortieth student to have stayed with them, the first Australian and by far the oldest. She revealed her love for her students when she said they were her children.

I will remember Amboise, not for its chateau, its history or its position in the Loire valley, but for the love and hospitality of my hosts, Danièle and Michele. I'll remember them for their kindness and compassion and for the bright fires of enthusiasm that burned within them. How wonderful it was to share my love for Maris and my grief for Joe with them. I felt nostalgic that I was in my bedroom for the last time. As sleep claimed me I felt close to Maris as if she was in the bed with me. I felt her footfalls in my heart. Her spirit would be my companion on the Way. Her spirit will always be my companion on my journey.

4. A thousand mile journey begins with a single step

Michele and Danièle were generous to the last. Along with Maya on Saturday morning they took me to the station and waited with me for the train. The first of many partings! I loved being part of their family and now I was back on my own. I felt lonely as I sat in the train barely noticing the French landscape flash by. My mind was back in Amboise, thinking of the many evenings we shared. In Paris I left the Gare Austerlitz and walked across the bridge to Gare de Lyon. As I settled into the TGV (*Train de grande vitesse*) my anxieties plagued me. I couldn't believe I was doing this! And at my age! Stepping out of one's comfort zone can be terrifying. How often have I been amazed at what I had let myself into?

I took out of my pocket the scallop shell which Danièle had given to me and ran my fingers along the grooves. These grooves came together at a single point and are supposed to represent the various routes the medieval pilgrims travelled, eventually arriving at the single destination, the tomb of St James. Danièle had conveniently drilled a hole in the base through which I threaded a piece of string and tied it to my backpack.

With the thought that it's too late to back out now, I changed trains at St Etienne and took a slow Rhône-Alps train to Le Puy-en-Velay. The train stopped all stations, rattled along the tracks through forests in contrast to the smooth rapid glide of the TGV through broad farmlands. There was plenty of room to spread out on the TGV but this one was a tight squash of people and backpacks. I guessed they were about to become pilgrims too. I looked over their faces – all young. I guessed I was the oldest.

Back in Australia I tried to book a bed via the internet but every establishment told me all the pilgrim accommodation was taken because of the festival and many folk would be returning to Le Puy. August 15th is the Feast of the Assumption. Not only was it a major feast day, it was also a public holiday. Eventually I was successful with the youth hostel. I had a long walk from the railway station, down through the modern city, then up the hill to the old town where the hostel was housed in an ancient building.

The cathedral was close to the hostel and Sunday morning I attended the 7.00 am Mass. Many had their backpacks and after the service everyone crowded on the steps of the porch for a pilgrims' blessing. I was one of about a hundred. The priest in charge asked where everyone came from. Most were French but other European countries were well represented. I was the only Australian. The chap next to me whispered in a very French accent, 'G'day, mate.'

We were given our *crédenciales*, a pilgrim's passport which was to be stamped every day at the places you pass through to prove that you were a pilgrim and to give you access to the general infrastructure of welcome. We were offered a basket in which visitors to the cathedral placed prayers of petition to Saint Jacques. Pilgrims were encouraged to take one and carry it all the way to Santiago. I took one, a mother praying for her wayward son. Most set off down the long flight of steps leading from the cathedral but I went back to the hostel for breakfast.

Not only was Sunday 15 August 2010 the Feast of the

Assumption, it was also the 150th anniversary of the feast of Our Lady Queen of France whose huge statue dominates the town, which gave the day a special importance in the French Catholic world. The weekend turned out to be the busiest of the year. Many former pilgrims were in town as well as devotees of Our Lady of France. Along with thousands of others I attended the Mass in the park which was so colourful with hundreds of flowerbeds if as they had been especially cultivated for the festival.

Twenty bishops concelebrated along with the cardinal archbishop of Paris. I was curious to sight the cardinal archbishop because his name is *Vingt-Trois*, which is twenty-three in English. What sort of person has a name like that? He turned out to be a little chap and he delivered a very patriotic homily on the virtues of France under the protection of Our Lady. Devotion to Mary, the mother of Jesus, is strong in France.

I rang Maria. She said she was coping okay, buoyed by the attention she had received. Her friends in the retirement village were being supportive but life seemed unreal as she hadn't got her head around the fact that Joe had gone and wouldn't be coming back. I told her I would ring her every few days and come to Queensland as soon as I returned to Australia.

I spent the day as a tourist. The *Cathédrale Notre-Dame du Puy* is striking. Sixty steps lead up to the porch with further steps up to the nave, followed by further steps into the nave and steps extending beyond. You seemed to be climbing all the while you are in the building.

Le Puy has been a pilgrimage centre since the Middle Ages, both as a starting point for French pilgrims and others from further fields en route to Santiago, and as a pilgrimage destination to Notre Dame in its own right. Le Puy is in a volcanic landscape dominated by rocky peaks rising from the valley floor.

One of the peaks is crowned by the chapel of Saint Michel

d'Aiguilhe. I climbed the 267 steps winding around the peak. How many millions had climbed the steep path before me? The other high point is the enormous statue of Notre Dame de France which overlooks the town from a rock high above. The statue was built in 1860 from Russian canons captured at Sebastopol during the Crimean War. I climbed inside the statue and peeped through the slit holes for a magnificent view of the town spread around the rocky peaks across the valley.

Monday morning I stood on the steps of the porch of the cathedral and looked beyond the town to the surrounding mountain ridges of the Haute-Loire and imagined beyond the horizon that Santiago and Saint James were waiting. I looked down the long flight of steps lined with blue and white bunting from the festival and the narrow street to which I was about to descend. I was petrified. My heart was pounding and my guts ached. I could smell my own sweat. My pilgrimage was about to start. How many millions before me had stood on these steps and experienced the same terror?

I had my pilgrim's blessing, Danièle's shell was on my back, and, armed with the knowledge that I was travelling under some kind of protection, I took my first step. I had often used the quotation of Lou-tzu, an ancient Chinese philosopher – *A thousand mile journey begins with a single step* – to encourage others to begin a difficult task. Here I was following my own advice, literally doing the same, taking the first step of a 1500 kilometres journey.

Armed with my guidebook I descended the steps, and walked down the narrow street, checking the guidebook's description against the actual ground and finding that they agreed. I was on the right track. A plaque announced that I was standing on the spot where was born the Via Podiensis, the great route of pilgrimage towards St Jacques de Compostelle.

Further on a signpost indicated 1521 kilometres to Santiago. The way was marked with the shell, a symbol which I was to find along the entire route. I saw the first of the small red and white stripes, an indicator for the GR 65. Thousands of kilometres of walking tracks cross France, known as *Grandes Randonnées*. The modern pilgrimage route through France follows one of these, the GR 65. These two symbols were to be my constant companions. They gave me great comfort when I saw them and disquiet when I didn't.

Once I was walking my nerves settled down. I became aware of the beauty of the morning – clear skies, a warm sun and light breeze. The day was made for walking. I passed the first of many images of Saint Jacques de Compostelle dressed in a pilgrim hat and cloak, holding his bourdon. The bourdon was the pilgrim's staff which, in medieval times, was considered a symbol of the spiritual support that the pilgrim received from Jesus.

I left the confines of the town and headed out into the country following a well-worn path. I came across the first of the wayside crosses. I was to pass hundreds of them. Some looked weather-beaten and could have been standing for centuries. Others looked as if erected in the last year or so. Passing pilgrims had placed small stones either on the base or on the arms of the cross. I too began a practice of finding a stone and placing it wherever there was room. An old tradition! Some pilgrims were penitents and were leaving their sins behind. Others were recognising the cross as a symbol of Christ, there to help them along the way. My stones acknowledged my passing. I had joined a huge community of brothers and sisters who had been passing by for up to one thousand years and who would continue to pass by in the years to come.

My guidebook suggested that I should walk 23.5 kilometres

to Saint-Privat-d'Allier. However, I had booked by internet into the *gîte* at Montbonnet, only sixteen kilometres. The *gîte d'étape* is for walkers and cyclists and usually contain dormitory-type accommodation. They are in walking distance of each other. I was giving myself an easy day. Famous last words!

I followed my guidebook directions closely. I was walking along a well formed path which followed the ridge line and the directions told me to take a track down the hill. A small shop was beside the track. I was tempted to stop and ask but instead I turned down that track. It didn't seem well used and eventually narrowed down to a footpath overgrown in patches with tall grass. Then the directions did not fit the surrounding. I was uneasy. I came across a road. The instructions said to pass by a low wall made of stones. I came across a stone wall and felt reassured although I realised I hadn't seen any guiding markers. It dawned on me that I had taken a wrong turn. I went into denial. The thought of climbing back up that rough track was too daunting. I came across more stone walls, which encouraged me. I arrived at a signpost pointing to Vale-près-le Puy. The name indicated that it was close to Le Puy. I was walking back to my starting point. What an idiot! I was filthy on myself for such a stupid mistake and swore at the sheep staring at me. My guidebook contained maps, so after I got over my frustration I sat down on one of the stone walls, worked out where I was, discovered Montbonnet and sorted out the roads I needed to follow.

The day steadily declined in excitement and vigour. Instead of sixteen kilometres, I walked an extra fourteen. The Camino was teaching me my first lessons. Always ensure that you have the route markers in sight. Those markers are a security blanket. If you see them, you are on track. If you don't, you're not. The second lesson is to travel lightly. I knew my pack was too heavy. With the excitement of a beginning, I didn't notice the weight, but as soon as I realised that I had to walk the extra kilometres, my pack weight increased dramatically. I fought off discouragement. I had hoped to ease myself into this pilgrimage game with a gentle first day. As the day grew hotter, a growing reluctance as well as my pack weighed me down. Its straps dug into my shoulders. The sun glared and burned my arms. I repeated the f word endlessly to the beat of my footsteps. I barely noticed my surroundings so intent was I on putting one foot in front of the other on the hot empty asphalt that reflected indifference to my suffering.

I had planned to arrive at the *gîte* by about 4.00 pm to give myself time for a shower and a rest. I rang the *gîte* to say I was definitely coming but I would be late. At 6.00 pm I was still on the road. The *gîte* rang me to see where I was. They would have to serve dinner without me. Pressure! My body was screaming for rest but I had to push on for another hour. I was scared I might collapse. I was barely able to drag one leg after another. With one last exhausting hill through the town, I clambered up to the *gîte*, just as everyone sat down to dinner.

I felt every one of my seventy-seven years, I was ashamed for getting myself lost. My shirt and shorts were saturated with sweat and I stank. At the end of the room the hostess served the meal from a huge pot. I was dirty and sweaty but she shouted a welcome and pointed to a place on one of the benches along the long wooden tables arranged in a U-shape. The tables were covered with bowls of salad, jugs of red wine and piles of baguettes. The guests near the pot passed the filled plates down the line. I gratefully accepted mine and realised I was hungry.

The beef casserole looked, smelt and tasted delicious. At first I was silent and discouraged, but was amazed how a good meal and a half litre of red wine revived my spirits. The people around me wanted to know where I was from and where I had started that day. I told my story of why I was late. Others spoke of their day of blisters; others laughed at the madness of what we were doing.

I looked around the tables at my fellow guests; about twenty, older men, young and mature women, young couples, mothers and daughters, sportsmen and the unfit, the spiritual and non-believers, all together sharing a meal, all on the same path. Some were walking only for the holidays, others were making for Jean-Pied-de-Port. One lady in her thirties was hoping to go all the way to Santiago by the end of October. I admired her skill as she carved her name with her pocketknife on her walking staff. Her name was Catherine. She carved each letter so slowly and perfectly and that evening got as far as H.

Later we shared the dormitories upstairs, baggage unpacked and contents strewn, all in together with no room for privacy. How I enjoyed stripping off my sweaty gear, stepping into the shower, the hot water streaming down my aching back and weary legs. I lingered over drying myself. It was a relief to be naked and unencumbered. I inspected my body in the mirror. My shoulders bore the marks of my backpack straps. My feet were sore and tender, but no blisters, thank God! I was thankful to climb into bed.

Why on Earth was I involved in such a caper, trekking across the French countryside with an overweight backpack? Why didn't I act my age and go on cruises and pass the time shuffling deckchairs? Apart from taking the wrong path, where had my spiritual journey led me? Up shit creek!

I learned a lot about myself on my first day. I heard the voice of a teacher. Was my Maris gently chiding me? Perhaps it was the Camino. The Camino has been teaching its pilgrims for a thousand years. Sometimes the lessons were so harsh that the pilgrim failed to live another day. I should have asked at that shop.

Firstly, did pride get in the way? I always want to work things out for myself, but sometimes one has to be humble and seek help. Secondly, I'm not a control freak, but I do like to be organised and plan ahead. I wanted to go easy on my first day. I should know by now that, although you might think you are in charge, any sense of direct control you think you might have over the world around you is almost all illusion. Events never turn out the way you want. If things are likely to go wrong, they will.

5. J'avance lentement mais surement

('I advance slowly but surely.')

In the morning my legs were stiff. I was weary, feeling seventy-seven-years-old, slow moving and late leaving the *gîte*. Inside, I was racing. Yesterday's failure had stirred something deep. Within us there's a quiet clear pool of strength, often hidden in the tangle of day-to-day activity, that we're not aware of it until we're challenged. I drank from that pool.

With grim and sober determination I extracted myself out of the brown creek and resolved to keep going. No setback was going to stop me. Hadn't I drawn on that same pool of strength and coped with the greatest of catastrophes when I lost Maris? Nothing worse could happen to me. I was vulnerable, at the mercy of the Camino and my own foolishness, but on my side, I had tenacity, Maris' spirit and an undefinable presence which I like to call God. In making my decision to continue, I felt stirrings in my internal journey. Just as I had matured spiritually in my handling of Maris' death, I would continue to grow spiritually in the face of any setbacks the Camino was likely to throw at me.

Suddenly what I had read made sense. The physical pilgrimage is a metaphor for an inner spiritual journey. It's like travelling through two parallel landscapes. The physical journey is always interwoven and in dialogue with the inner spiritual journey.

Once I had sorted myself out, I rang to reserve a bed. In France you book ahead. You decide how far you want to walk that day and contact a *gîte* in that town or village and usually you are asked whether you want the *demi-pension* which covers dinner, bed and breakfast.

The day was beautiful – cloudless and warm. I was climbing steadily, ensuring I kept the markers in sight. The route passed by ancient stone buildings, through forests and open ground, wound around valleys and rolling hills offering magnificent views of the rivers and villages below, of a patchwork of green fields interspersed with woodlands, the only sounds the birds chirping and the wind stirring the trees. In my solitude I forget my tired legs and the weight on my back. Yesterday I didn't take much notice of the world around me, but today I was aware. I felt uplifted. I was in awe of God's creation. I did not regard this natural world as something to observe or control.

I've long believed from my bushwalking days that wilderness is not expendable, nor the natural world an object for humans to consume. It is for our reverence and we must do our best to preserve it. I belong to environmental organisations and am distressed when I read of clear felling old growth forests for wood chipping. I've never chained myself to a bulldozer but I joined in spirit those activists who protested on behalf of those who believe that, when creation is damaged, they themselves are damaged.

The French countryside is as beautiful as the Australian bush. France has the advantage of a heavier rainfall but its appeal is just as moving. Walking, moving slowly made me part of this landscape. I was part of creation and at the same time creation was part of me. Being on foot sharpens the senses. You see, hear, feel and smell everything, so different to when you flash by in a car.

I had to rest frequently for the hills were gruesome. I was to find that every hill was a challenge. I saw Monistrol nestling by the river in a valley below me. I was tired, aching, hot and sweaty by the time I descended, hopeful of no more hills after a tough day but the toughest hill was saved for the last, the one leading up through the village to the *gîte*, the *Gîte d'étape La Tsabone*.

I arrived about 5.00 pm and was warmly welcomed by the young hostess. The *gîte* was small with beds for ten. I had my shower and washed my sweat saturated clothes. It's amazing how a shower and a rest can revive a weary pilgrim. Arriving earlier allowed me time to enjoy the evening. Six of the guests were from the one family, brothers, sisters, cousins in their fifties and sixties. They lived in various parts of France but came together to walk the Camino for two weeks. They had no plans to ever reach Santiago and seemed impressed when I said that was my eventual destination.

Among the other guests was Catherine from the previous night. While waiting for dinner, she carved more of her name on her walking staff, accompanied by lots of advice from the family of six.

They all had their walking sticks of the expandable variety. I was interested for I had never used a stick in my bushwalking but they vouched for their usefulness, to help you get up and down hills and also to ward off unwelcome dogs. They demonstrated how the height could be altered to suit the walker's height and the terrain.

The young hostess served a delicious chicken casserole dish made from produce from their own farm just out of the town. The ten of us sat on benches around a single wooden table. All were French. I was the stranger but felt at home. The night was full of laughter, jokes and songs. It was easy to forget the pain of the day after a shower and fresh clothes, but when you add good food, a few glasses of red and jovial conversation, the suffering never existed.

This is what evenings on the Camino should be like, I thought as I went to bed happy, in contrast to the previous night when I arrived late, disoriented and ashamed for getting lost. My body was tired but standing up to the pressure, as yet no blisters although my back ached with the weight of my backpack. I sorted my belongings into necessary items and stuff that I could do without and resolved that I would send the surplus back to Australia. I was applying the Camino's first lesson: *Travel lightly*.

I woke Wednesday morning refreshed and enthused but the stuffing was knocked out of me by a confronting climb of four kilometres as soon as I left the town, a killer hill if ever there was one, with a rope fence that the feeble pilgrim could cling to. I had to stop many times and admire the view below of Monistrol, a tiny patch of civilisation in a wilderness, clinging to the river crossed by two long bridges. I met the family of six, struggling up the steep incline. They seemed to be making full use of their sticks; some had two to help them up the hill. *Perhaps, I could use them*, I thought. From the walkers' exhausted facial expressions, I could tell I was not alone. I felt a bond with my fellows.

I arrived at Saugues about 2.30 pm. I had only walked about thirteen kilometres but that was more than enough. My back was aching and my shoulders were sore. My first task was to visit the Post Office where I purchased a box and filled it with five kilograms. My pack still felt heavy as I made my way to the night's accommodation. Once you are tired, your pack is never light. You long to get the encumbrance off your back.

I had reserved a bed at the *Centre d'accueil La Margeride*, a long low building which seemed to have accommodation for hundreds. I was placed in a room for three. The hosts were warm, welcoming and efficient, used to dealing with large numbers and having their systems to follow. After a shower and washing I visited the church and lit two candles, the first of many, and found a quiet bar up a side street where I enjoyed a couple of beers.

The family of six came by and joined me. I enjoyed their chatter. The dining room had several tables and lots of diners, including a number of children. I wasn't sure where to sit but the family of six invited me to join them. The meal was good but the staff were intent on getting their job done quickly. The larger accommodation did not have the same ambiance. Another Camino lesson! If you want atmosphere, stay at the small *gîtes* in the villages rather than the towns.

Back in my room I chatted in both English and French with Boris, a roommate, a young man in his twenties. He lived at Lyon and was walking for two weeks. He hoped to return each year in his holidays and eventually arrive at Santiago. He was keen to know my age and when I told him I was planning to reach Santiago, he expressed admiration and hoped that he would have my attitude when he was my age. I must admit I felt humble to think that my story inspired him. I felt for Boris. He seemed troubled. I sensed he could suffer from depression but he did not open up to me. Not that I expected him, but my years of living with Maris who suffered depression has alerted me to its possible presence in the people I meet.

Next morning as I walked alone I reflected on my fellow pilgrims. I was placing my feet in the footprints of those who had preceded me since the middle ages and even before that. I was joining others who, like me, had left home, leaving everything behind, coming on foot and some on bicycle, alone, in groups, in couples. Throughout history, people of all religions and cultures have been undertaking pilgrimages. They leave their world, lose their social status, and become strangers in an unfamiliar land.

In the Middle Ages, people went on pilgrimages mostly for religious reasons. Some went as a profession of faith. For others it was a form of punishment. My guidebook tells me that at one stage there was in operation a system of fixed penalties for certain sins, like today's mandatory sentencing. Others saw their pilgrimage as a means of atonement or as a way of acquiring merit, reducing the amount of time spent in Purgatory. Some wanted to venerate the relics of many saints available along the route to Santiago as indulgences were available to those who visited shrines. Others, perhaps, were bored witless and just wanted to escape their tedious surroundings.

My solitude was crowded for there were many walkers on the road, all warm in their greeting. I heard countless 'Bon Chemin' and 'Bonne Route'. These greetings gave others the encouragement to go on not only with the Camino but at another level with life. I was amazed how quickly you formed a bond with people despite the different languages as you walked with them for a time or chatted at a resting point. Most were French, but there were Germans and Swiss with the occasional English.

People were interested in where others had come from. They were interested in me, all the way from Australia. They asked how long I had been walking and where I was planning to reach. I asked the same questions of them. Some were walking the whole way to Santiago but others were walking the Camino in stages. Some had walked the route several times. They had been compelled to return.

The hills were not of the lethal variety but there were plenty of them, gradually ascending into high country. I reached Le Villeret d'Apcher in about five hours where I had booked into the *Gîte d'étape L'Auberge des deux pèlerins*. This *gîte* had strict rules forbidding boots and packs from the rooms, an attempt to minimise the introduction of bed bugs, a problem on the Camino.

Jean-Louis did everything loudly but he was a generous host. He conducted a happy hour on the terrace before dinner on a beautifully balmy evening and with his guitar led us guests in a number of songs about the Camino. He handed out song sheets. Jean-Louis and his wife Lucette had formerly been pilgrims although by the size of Jean-Louis' tummy, it could have been some time ago.

At dinner he introduced each course as if he were staging a theatre production. The main meal was aligot, a regional dish consisting of cheese and potato. He produced a large bowl of a very viscous mixture and delighted in spooning the contents up to a height and allowing it to fall back in the dish. He served each guest with a similar flourish. He hit the plate every time. He introduced each cheese with a description of its nature and origin. Similarly, he brought out a range of liqueurs, brandies and ports, gave a description of each and invited each guest to make his or her choice. Jean-Louis was a showman who revelled in his guests' attention but he was a catalyst for an excellent night of lively conversation.

Next to me sat Martin, a French Canadian sporting a Camino tattoo. He had completed the Camino in Spain and was now following the route from Le Puy. He had plans to do a number of the routes through Western Europe. Three of the family from the previous night were at my table; the others had gone home. People were curious about me and asked a predictable set of questions. They listened to my French and guessed I was German. When I answered I was Australian they expressed surprise that I had come so far.

They asked how come I spoke fluent French. I didn't think I was that fluent. I often had to struggle with both the correct vocabulary and grammar, always having to search for the proper conjugation of the verbs, and remember the gender of the nouns, which then determined the agreement of the adjectives, to say nothing of the form of irregular verbs. I had the understanding that, such is their devotion to the language, that the French demand to hear it spoken well and hate hearing it massacred. I formed the impression on this and many other evenings over dinner that the French people appreciated my speaking their language. The French love their language and defend their culture against the oppressive onslaught of English's domination of the world. I was thankful that I have adequate French to pitch into the conversation. Otherwise, I could have been a lonely old man waiting for some kind person who spoke English to include me.

I shared a room with a family. Antoine and Anna were from Paris. They were walking the Camino with their young family. Jude was twelve but the two girls were younger. The room was in two parts, three beds in each. Anna and the girls slept in the other part while Antoine, Jude and I shared. Antoine was interested in my life as I was in his. He worked for a company that exported fine tableware, including to Australia. Although he knew English he chose to speak in French. We chatted. Jude listened and asked the occasional question about Australia. He knew about kangaroos. He was interested in my coming from the other side of the world. I went to sleep thankful that I had chosen to stay in this tiny village with such good company. In the morning Antoine had to wake Jude. He sat up, rubbed his eyes and the first thing he said was, 'Bonjour, Noël.' In his simple greeting I felt complete acceptance.

I continued the steady climb on another fine day, through more beautiful French countryside, with its patchwork of forest and farms. In fact, the route often went through clusters of stone farm buildings with their cows and sheep and geese. The cows and sheep were indifferent to passers-by but the geese weren't so friendly and were ever ready to flap their wings and defend their patch against these invaders in walking boots. I met Antoine and his family with another cheery 'Bonjour, Noël' from Jude. I was surprised that many walkers remembered my name. I was different, the elderly Australian on his own who could speak French.

A sign post indicated I had 1478 kilometres to reach Santiago. I enjoyed the message written on the signpost – *'J'avance lentement mais surement'* (I advance slowly but surely) – with a crude drawing of a snail. This simple piece of graffiti described my sentiments. I was not in a race to get to the destination as quickly as possible. I was taking my time, making sure that I had the time to look around me and enjoy the countryside. My spirit was in touch with the earth and with the ambience of the Camino. I mentioned that graffiti to a lady who walked with me for a while as we passed through a pine forest. She taught me a proverb: *'Rien ne sert de courir; it faut partir à point.'* Its literal translation is, 'There's no sense in running; you just have to leave on time.' But it's the French equivalent of 'Slow and steady wins the race.'

Rather than stay in the town of Saint-Alban-sur-Limagnole I chose a *gîte* on a farm, *Gîte d'étape à la Ferme La Croix du Plo* at Le Rouget just short of the town. The *gîte* was part of a large barn or *hangar*. At one end was the accommodation, at the other were the cows and in between hundreds of hay bales stacked to the roof. You had to walk through the *hangar* and up some stairs to get to the *gîte*.

There were nine guests – six ladies and three men. There was a moment of tension when one of the ladies who arrived later couldn't get her head around the notion of sleeping in a room with a man (me!), so, although people had already selected their beds, some negotiation took place until everyone was resettled. I shared a room with two ladies who weren't so fussy. Sleeping arrangements in the *gîtes* would never suit privacy freaks.

The evening turned out well with lots of chatter over a dinner provided by the farmer's wife from the farm's produce. Everyone was French. I had to answer the usual questions. Breakfast was just as noisy as dinner.

On the way out, I passed the farmer busy spreading hay. He was a jovial fresh faced young man who stopped feeding his cows for a chat. I was pleased that I had stayed the night on a farm, surrounded by rural silence. I continued to pass through beautiful agricultural countryside. I felt a deep affinity. I loved the silence and the solitude and found myself expressing thanks to be part of God's creation. The landscape made up for the killer hills. I had to pause many times but at the same time, I was absorbing and being part of my surroundings. The only sounds were the birds, the cow bells and an occasional chime from a distant church. I gave thanks that I was alive, that I was fit and healthy. I was walking across France when many people of my age couldn't walk across the room. I was on my sixth day of walking and so far my body had coped. No blisters!

At Saint Alban sur-Limagnole I visited the church of Saint Etienne and lit candles. As I sat in front of the altar, I realised the day was Saturday and the time was 9.20 am, just after the time on Saturday 30 October 2004 that Maris had left home saying she was going to visit a friend to exchange some books.

My mind raced through the events of that day, my sense
of dread, the arrival of the police, the visit to the Royal North
Shore Hospital, the young doctor telling us the news and the
identification of her body. I grieved and suffered in my body,
in my heart and in my spirit. I wept quietly in that dark church
as I watched the candles burning. They would burn for the
day and prolong my prayer. There was a message of hope in
those candles because after a catastrophe there comes a period
when life continues, the heart is regenerated and the spirit is
renewed. I felt fragile that day and left two stones on every
wayside cross. If I couldn't light candles I would leave stones
instead. The day was full of hills. I was slow but persistent.
Everyone passed me but I reached the top. I read graffiti by
the artist with the snail signature.

'*Le temps n'est rien.*' (Time is nothing.)

I like that artist. He was taking his time just as I was. I
didn't impose a pressure on myself to get as far as I could in a
limited time. I knew how much time I had and if I didn't reach
Saint-Jean-Pied-de-Port, I would come back later. I loved the
sense of timelessness. I couldn't remember exactly where I'd
been the day before, but, paradoxically, I could remember the
detail of each place very well. Moving constantly and at such
a slow pace, time stretched out before me. I felt as though I
had limitless time to get to my destination. I had downshifted
from modern speed to medieval speed, to mankind's slowest
form of transportation – walking. I might cross a road and see
a car speeding past, hitting me in the face with exhaust fumes,
and know that where that car would be in an hour would take
me five or six days. Or a jet might pass overhead and cover
several hundred kilometres in the same time. Today's world
spins faster and faster; an email can travel around the globe
in a fraction of a second. As you move under the hot sun, you

sweat out the stresses of modern life and, instead of worrying about the next thing you should do, you note the course of the sun, the length of the shadows, the passage of clouds, the sound of the wind and the birds.

I arrived in Aumont-Aubrac at my chosen *gîte, le gîte d'étape La Ferme du Barry.* I shared a room with five ladies, including the ladies of the previous night. Our host Vincent was just as flamboyant with his aligot as Jean-Louis back at Villaret d'Apcher. He stretched his long arm to the ceiling and the aligot hung like a long strand of spaghetti before falling back to the bowl. He served each guest's plate with similar flamboyance. He explained how aligot was made and produced the blocks of cheese used in the recipe. After dinner Vincent allowed me to access the internet. I sent emails to the family and checked the Australian news. The federal election held that day was a cliff-hanger. If I had been in Australia, I would have been absorbed, but here on the timeless Camino, the news seemed to belong to an arrogant world where everyone is out to perform, achieve, compete and destroy the other.

My wise teacher, the Camino, was giving me another lesson: *Slow down, take your time, value what matters.*

6. Dans le silence et la solitude, on n'entend plus que l'essentiel

('In the silence and solitude
one hears only the essentials')

Aumont-Aubrac is the beginnings of the Aubrac, a large plateau which, for the pilgrims, requires a degree of caution. A semi-desert region, it is a land of many risks. In ancient times, the pilgrim had to run the gauntlet of wolves and brigands. In modern times, the pilgrim is warned not to try crossing in bad weather or storms. Early snowfalls are expected and strong winds can whip across the flat grasslands. One cannot expect to see much beyond stone walls and extensive grasslands battered by rough weather.

I was fortunate in that I encountered hot but calm conditions. The plateau rises to 1200 metres, which meant I had climbed 600 metres since leaving Le Puy.

I paused at La Chaze-de-Peyre where I entered the church and lit my two candles. In the church was one other pilgrim. Standing in the middle of the nave, she was singing loudly and seemed to be lost in her song. Her dress was equally eccentric in that she wore a long kaftan which I thought was not very suitable for walking. I thought no more of her as I left the church other than each person has his or her way of doing the Camino.

I walked on my own on this open, silent landscape; even the birds were quiet. The path zigzagged as it followed fences lines made of stones. I admired the waves and patterns that the breeze made on the grasslands. I stopped for lunch at a bar in the middle of nowhere. The place was Les Quartes Chemins and the bar was *Chez Régine*. I sat under an awning where Régine served me drinks and a sandwich. I gave some crumbs to Régine's chooks and dogs wandering around my feet under the table.

Shortly after leaving *Chez Régine* I came across an older couple eating a picnic lunch. They introduced themselves as Chris and John Martin. They had been to the market at Aumont Aubrac and were on their way back to Saint-Côme-d'Olt where they had the house next to the *boulangerie*. They were an English couple and lived in Derbyshire but had a house in France for the summer. I welcomed the opportunity to speak in English. Before taking my leave John mentioned I would reach Saint-Côme-d'Olt in a few days and was welcome to call in.

My accommodation for the evening was called *Les Gentianes*, attached to a farm on its own in the country. *Les Gentianes* consisted of a restaurant, *gîte d'étape* and a *chambre d'hôtes*. If you were a pilgrim and looking for a cheap bed in a shared room, you selected the *gîte d'étape*, but if you wanted to go up market and have a private room you chose the *chambre d'hôtes*.

Everyone dined in the restaurant. The restaurant was at the front while the *gîte*, like an afterthought, was down the back near a *hangar* full of fodder bales. There was one other guest, Catherine, who had completed carving her name on her stick. Quite a few beds were empty, which was unusual because up to now every *gîte* had been full.

After washing myself and my clothes I ambled back to the front and sat outside with a beer. Along came the lady I met singing in the church at La Chaze-de-Peyre, tired and dishevelled, her hair everywhere, looking for a bed. I knew there were plenty of beds back at the *gîte* but the hostess told her she had none. The lady accepted the decision and said she would walk on to the next place. I felt sorry and indignant for her and was tempted to ask the hostess why she knocked her back. Perhaps she didn't like her eccentric appearance. I decided to reserve judgment. Perhaps she already had reservations and was waiting for the people to arrive. They never did. This was a problem for the *gîtes*. One had to ring ahead to make reservations but people often did not turn up or ring to cancel. The host has to turn away people who could have had a bed. Some reserve beds at several *gîtes* and don't bother to cancel the others. How inconsiderate!

I chatted to Catherine, keen to know how she had fared since I saw her last. She had to pause for a day because she had suffered blisters and needed some time out. She told me she would have to push on if she wanted to reach Santiago within her time frame. She cooked her own dinner but I dined in the restaurant. I joined two couples, guests in the *chambre d'hôtes* for the pilgrim menu. I didn't regard my fellow diners as pilgrims. They were on a walking holiday and had their baggage carried each day from stage to stage. I did not feel the same bond or sense of camaraderie with them as I did with those who carried everything on their backs and were prepared to suffer hardships, discomforts and lack of privacy. Nevertheless, I enjoyed their company and they were just as curious about my motivation. The same question: *Why had I come all the way from Australia and at my age?*

Les Gentianes is very close to Finieyrols where, the following morning, I passed a monument celebrating the birthplace of Louis Dalle. The inscription described him as being born in 1922, the thirteenth of fifteen children. In 1944 he was deported to Buchenwald. After the war he became a missionary in Peru and eventually a bishop. I passed the house where he was born and an inscription gave more details. At Buchenwald he suffered so much that he could not stand suffering in others. He gave the gift of himself to his fellow inmates and somehow survived. He regarded his time at Buchenwald as a blessing. His suffering made him free. He dedicated his life to defending the people of the Andes in Peru against deceit and injustice.

I hadn't heard of Louis Dalle, but I liked him. I compared his life with that of Victor Frankel. Like Louis Dalle he survived a concentration camp during World War II. He, too, experienced suffering but emerged with his humanity intact. He wrote in his book, *Man's Search for Meaning*, that people can endure immense suffering if they can find some purpose in their experience. It can be difficult to find meaning in suffering when there is no hope of relief but, sometimes, the meaning lies simply in how one bears one's condition. We cannot always control our circumstances but we can control our attitudes towards them. We have a choice to retain our humanity and that freedom cannot be taken away from us.

Strange! In the middle of this barren landscape, my encounter with Louis Dalle led me to another way of looking at suffering in my life. There's nothing wonderful about suffering when you're in the midst of it. You want to get out of it. When you see a pattern or direction, you can accept it and go with it. To survive is to find meaning in the suffering. I loved my wife so deeply that my grief was equally profound. I could have succumbed to bitterness and despair, but I looked for a deeper meaning in my suffering, chose to live and used my own experience to reach out to others who have been similarly bereaved, a task about which I have become quite passionate. Without the loss of my wife Maris, I would not have reached out to these people nor gone on this pilgrimage. Perhaps this was another lesson the Camino was teaching me. Out of suffering emerges strength. I had seen suffering in my fellow pilgrims. Many who had experienced severe blisters still chose to continue.

I stopped for lunch at Nasbinals and lit two candles in the church. In the silence I felt a presence. As I looked deeply into myself I left the lighted candles behind and seemed to gaze into an inner light. I felt this presence like a life force that connected me with everyone that has ever been born and who would be born. I imagined the presence was like an engine room, the same source of power for me and every creature.

I left the candles behind to prolong my prayer and continued walking along the plateau to Aubrac. According to my guidebook, Aubrac was founded in 1120 by a Flemish knight who was attacked by bandits on his way to Santiago and on the way home almost perished in a storm. In gratitude, for his deliverance he founded Aubrac as a refuge for pilgrims.

My refuge was a bed at the *Les Gîtes de Royal Aubrac* at the edge of town. The site contained a curious collection of buildings. Next to the *gîte* was a large unoccupied multi-story building, now abandoned. I was told it was formerly a mental hospital.

The *gîte*, like a motel, was formerly staff quarters where I had a room of my own. The area was spooky, as if old ghosts were hanging around. I wondered why the mental hospital was abandoned but there was no one to ask. The lady who booked me in had disappeared. I found the place depressing. It smelt of neglect. The enormous kitchen was probably the staff dining room. No evening meal was available. I felt too tired to walk into town to one of the restaurants. Instead I had a meal of bread, cheese and a banana.

The evening on my own was very quiet. In this silence I

was looking forward to a long deep restful sleep but I had an uncomfortable night for my right knee ached. The worry of having to stay a day or two until my knee was better in this miserable spot kept me awake. I might have to abandon the pilgrimage – my great fear.

In the morning my knee was okay. I chastised myself for making a catastrophe out of nothing and set out for the day. This was my eighth day on the Camino. I had walked 128 kilometres and had more than 500 to get to the Pyrenees. The days had merged into a continuous movement of sun and rain, mountains and plains, forests and farms, thirst and fatigue, hunger and sleep.

I had settled into a simple routine. The pilgrim's life is simplicity itself – walking, carrying the basics, washing clothes by hand, eating from a pilgrims' menu or cooking for one's self, sleeping in dormitories, sharing stories with other pilgrims. In this simplicity I'd broken away from modern compulsions for collecting more material goods, preoccupations with comfort and privacy and found the unacknowledged spirituality of life – values such as a sense of the present, good company and connection with the natural world. Life was following an ancient rhythm. The simplicity led me to an internal peace, my main concern each day being a bed for the night. The simple act of walking had given me the time to look around me to admire nature and to feel part of it. It was like getting back to basics.

I passed a monument:

Dans le silence et la solitude, on n'entend plus que l'essentiel.

(In the silence and the solitude one hears only the essential).

That simple piece of wisdom was close to the core of my spiritual journey. In the silence and solitude of long distance walking, I hoped I might hear a small voice, asking a big question like, *What's the deeper meaning of my life?*

I hoped I might feel closer to God, whatever God was. Again and again, in different religions and in different ways and with different languages mankind has struggled with the idea of a Divine reality. The goal of human existence was to be united with that Reality. It's hard to get a handle on God. Many people have given up trying.

I was raised as a Catholic at a time when prescribed beliefs weren't questioned and obedience to authority trumped following one's conscience. We were taught to live behind closed doors of fear. Many Catholics have dumped their religious upbringing totally but I like to believe I've learned to think critically, to ask questions and have identified what is spiritually vital to me. I like to think my journey had led me away from fear to a reasoned faith while still staying on track in the Catholic tradition, which has some wonderful messages about human dignity and social justice.

(I have to admit, however, that, if the Catholic Church had still maintained its stance towards suicides, such as refusing to bury them in 'sacred ground', I'd no longer be a Catholic.)

Beyond the doctrine, there was something that was eternal, wild, transcendent, immense, mysterious and unknowable, that words could not adequately describe nor our minds comprehend. I didn't want to settle for easy certitudes, for a small god instead of a Big Mystery. Could I emerge from the Camino as a different Noel, changed forever through an encounter with this Something? In the silence and the solitude would I hear only the essentials?

I had decided to make for Saint-Côme-d'Olt, which was

twenty-five kilometres, and took a punt that it would be downhill all the way. I set out in mist which turned into rain and so used my wet weather gear for the first time. My punt paid off. I walked downhill all the way with a few smaller hills. I descended 900 metres and took seven hours to walk the twenty-five kilometres. By the time I reached Saint-Côme-d'Olt on the river Lot the weather had cleared and the evening was fine.

I loved this village. Delightfully medieval, it had few modern buildings. Olt is the old name for the river Lot. I found the communal *gîte* in an ancient building, once a prison. The *gîte* was basic but I had a great view across the rooftops to the church. I found a chap in the kitchen waiting to take the money and he directed me up the stairs to a room with six bunks.

One of them was occupied by a teenage boy surrounded by empty soft drink cans and chip wrappers. He stared at me all the time as if I were the enemy and although I tried to make conversation he said and did nothing other than stare as if he were a trapped animal ready for fight or flight. I was wary, too, as I didn't know his story or whether he was a threat. Passive aggression oozed out of his skin. If he became violent, I'd be the loser. I gave up trying to communicate and went downstairs to do a quick tour of the village.

On the way outside, the chap taking the money asked, 'Is the boy still in the room?'

'Yes.'

'He shouldn't be there,' he said. 'Not to worry, I'll get rid of him.'

I had my wallet, camera and passport with me, my most valuable items. I was stupid to leave my pack in the room but decided the contents were replaceable should the boy help himself before his eviction. I returned to find the room empty and my pack untouched. I was curious about the boy's story, but I never found out.

I thought of doing the simple pilgrim thing and cook a meal in the communal kitchen, but decided I could afford a meal in the village's only restaurant. The restaurant was expensive. No pilgrim's menu here! They were catering for the well-heeled tourists, of which there were plenty. The night was warm so I explored the town before returning to the *gîte*. I found a *boulangerie* and wondered on which side lived my English friends Chris and John Martin, whom I met eating their picnic lunch a few days previously.

I slept until 8.00 am as I had no early risers to disturb me. On my way out of town I visited the church, lit two candles and ran into John Martin. He had spotted me walking across the square and followed me into the church. He invited me for a cup of tea at his house which was next to a *boulangerie* but not the one I passed the night before. I spent an enjoyable hour sipping tea with this English couple.

They bought the house about thirty years previously, a derelict at the time and spent years in renovation. They enjoyed showing before and after photos and took me on a tour. The house was messy but comfortable and had a great feel of cosiness. They spent about six weeks each year at the house which they left in their absence in the care of the *boulanger* next door. He used the unused rooms to store his flour. I left late morning and Chis and John walked with me to the gothic bridge at the edge of town. I was delighted to have met such a couple and their simple generosity invigorated me for the day.

I had the option of an easy walk along the Lot River but, the masochist that I am, I chose the harder, longer way and walked over the hill. The path was steep and difficult and at

the top a statue of the Virgin looked out over the landscape.
From this lofty platform the view along the river back to Saint-
Côme-d'Olt and forward to Espalion was an excellent prize
for my exertion. Back at the river Lot I had lunch feeding the
ducks. My destination was Espalion further along the river.
As it came into view, ancient buildings lined the edge of the
water. I crossed over an arched pilgrim bridge said to be a
thousand-years-old to stay at the *Gîte d'étape La Halte Saint
Jacques*. Checking in was done at the adjacent bar/restaurant
where the pilgrim menu dinner was served.

I was sitting outside the restaurant enjoying a beer prior to
the meal and watched the people emerge over the hump of the
bridge – first their heads appeared, then finally their bodies.

A young woman arrived. She was distressed and asked the
lady in the restaurant to be taken to the gendarmerie. Her
name was Jane and she was English with little French so I
helped with the translation. She was embarrassed and reluctant to give details at first but she eventually said that she had
been sexually assaulted. When pressed for details, she said a
man had 'flashed' himself. Jane wanted to report the incident.
I felt for Jane. I could see how shaken she was. I wanted to
help, offered to go with her but the lady of the house took Jane
and returned to serve the meal. After the meal I went for a
walk and leaned over the bridge and admired the sun setting
on the water and fishermen silhouetted in the fading light. I
wondered how Jane was faring when she walked by.

'Did you get a good hearing?' I asked.

'Yes, the gendarmes listened,' she replied. 'Such incidents
are common, they said. Offenders drive to a place where the
Camino crosses a road and wait for women on their own. One
offender they know of drives a green Renault.'

This darker side of the Camino disturbed me. I had observed

the odd car parked on a road by the path but hadn't taken notice. I'd look out for them now, particularly green Renaults. By now Jane had overcome her shock and was angry. She wanted to take to the offender with her pocket knife and chop off his penis. She gave me a demonstration of how she would do it. We found a bar and had a quiet drink together. She was calm when we parted.

As I faded into sleep that night my thoughts were about cars parked in lonely spots. The Camino is regarded as safe but I thought of the safety of the many young women walking alone. In medieval times physical dangers were abundant, but in modern times incidents appear to be uncommon. No doubt there are thieves on the Camino as there are anywhere.

It was early as I walked away from Espalion but already the air was beginning to shimmer with heat. Along the river, which hugged the edge of the town, ducks swam and the tree boughs swayed and dipped into the water.

Three kilometres beyond Espalion I rounded a bend and the Church of Saint Pierre de Bessuéjouls, one of the oldest churches along the route, appeared through the tree-lined track. As I turned and approached, I could see its slowly crumbling edifice, but there was still a sense of awe which must have inspired its early worshipers.

Inside it was cool and dark, and at the far end was a simple altar that had been standing since the 9th century. I climbed the bell tower and found the chapel of Saint-Michel, which dates back to the 11th century. Inside the entrance was a table with copies of a *Guide Spirituel du Pèlerin*. I left money for a copy. Every now and then I could read a prayer or reflection.

Outside I sat on the steps of a large weathered stone cross and flicked through my *Guide*. Along came Jane walking with an older woman. She was in good spirits and I was pleased she had chosen not to walk alone. Her companion was German and seemed a feisty lady who knew how to look after herself. Jane was in good hands.

The day grew hotter and the sun was becoming as lethal as the hills. I had to rest at the top of every rise and used half of my water, tipping it over my head. I was dry by the time I resumed walking.

It was a day that would test the hardiest. Although Estaing was just over twelve kilometres from Espalion, that was more than enough for such a day.

I checked the souvenir shop for my booking at the communal *gîte*. The heat bounced off the walls as I clung to the narrow band of shadow and made my way up the hill to the *gîte*. By the bodies lying on beds and belongings strewn everywhere I guessed everyone was exhausted. Their drawn faces indicated they were on the point of collapse, ready to give away this crazy Camino business. I'm dead sure everyone longed for air-conditioned comfort, but the *gîte* was housed in a former chapel and the beds were in airless cubicles just under the roof. The lack of windows made the dormitory stifling. Only one door at the end caught any breeze. My shower was temporary relief from the heat and perspiration. It was a day to drink plenty of water.

I was intrigued by one group. They sat down to an early dinner of soup. I had noticed one of the men making the soup with greens. That's all they had – soup and water. One told me they were on the Camino for five days living on the soup. He gave me a taste. It was okay but I could not imagine being sustained for five days just on soup.

'Why are you only having soup? I asked.

The chap had difficulty explaining or I had difficulty understanding but it was something to do with diet and spirituality and cleansing the body and spirit of impurities. Most of the others went out to dine at a restaurant, but I decided it was time to do the simple pilgrim thing and cook pasta for myself. I spent the evening chatting with a French girl and an older German. Gaëlle from Normandy was finishing in a few days. The holidays were about to end and she was going back to her work as a teacher. Her feet were painted red with antiseptic. She offered me the last of the antiseptic as well as plasters and safety pins.

The older German, Dieter, spoke excellent English and was rather serious and intense. He wanted to discuss the spirituality of the Camino. I sensed that he was searching and suggested that spirituality meant many things to people but the Camino might help some deal with questions related to the deeper meaning of their lives. The solitude of walking can be a time for reflection.

This stimulated him to talk about his own life. He felt lonely and abandoned after his wife died. He struggled with his Catholic religious upbringing and drifted away from church attendance. He felt he was in a vacuum.

I said that you could be spiritual without being religious. Religion was about a set of beliefs. You belong to a religion. Developing your spiritual life is an individual thing and can give you a sense of purpose and help you figure out where you are most passionate in your life.

We got on to the role of suffering in our lives and how one can grow spiritually as a result. He spoke of his wife's death by cancer and I told him of Maris' suicide and how I now work with other people who have lost a loved one to suicide. I mentioned passing the memorials to Louis Dalle back at Finieyrols. He regarded his suffering as a gift which enabled him to attend to the suffering of others.

Dieter said he continued to believe in God and asked if I did.

I replied yes but I had to qualify my answer and asked Dieter for the patience to hear me out. For me God has always been a slippery character. Just as you feel you are getting somewhere, things fade away. I told Dieter that, like him, I was reared in the Catholic tradition and had accepted the ready-made set of solutions of my church.

In later years, I began to question beliefs and although I hadn't rejected them all by any means, I found myself in doubt. I said that this doubt gave me a creativity and passion to inquire. I was prepared to move out of my comfort zone, to leap into the unknown. I saw faith as a journey into darkness, into the unknown. Faith allows us to trust in answers that are best guesses. If we knew all the answers there would be no need for trust and faith. There would be no need for pilgrimages.

Dieter was a patient listener. He was keen to hear more so in I plunged. I told him that in my university studies in psychology I learned about scientific method and looking at issues with the 'eyes of science'. Nowadays I find the phrase 'the eyes of faith' useful. When trying to explain an event or phenomenon one can look at it with the eyes of science or with the eyes of faith. With the eyes of science you look for a logical or rational explanation of why things are so. You may look at the same event with the eyes of faith and this opens the possibility of God's hand at work. Both outlooks are complementary. They don't have to contradict each other.

My training in scientific method causes me to think in terms of working hypotheses in arriving at solutions to life's problems. You evaluate what you already know of a situation and develop a working hypothesis which enables you to work with a particular explanation of an event and to take action. The hypothesis explains why things are so, and will do until a better explanation comes along as more information or knowledge comes to light.

I paused to pour us each a red wine. What a picture we presented! The night's heavy heat closed in upon us – two old blokes in earnest discussion facing each other across the wooden table, both in singlet and shorts, the perspiration falling off our pickled faces. I stumbled on.

One of my working hypotheses is that God exists. I'd probably act and live out my life in the same way if my belief in God was rock solid, if I was absolutely dead certain that God existed. Like any hypothesis, it's open to questioning and it is possible that another explanation may come along. Up to now, I haven't come across any evidence that will make me alter my working hypothesis.

I apologised to Dieter for answering his question in such a long-winded manner. He thanked me for taking the time to talk to him. I was exhausted by having to think deeply on such a stifling night and was grateful when the people returned from their restaurant and I joined them with a few more red wines. It was a night to anaesthetise oneself with alcohol for the heat continued and people were restless. No one slept.

My evening at Estaing was memorable, not only for its heat but for my interactions with Gaëlle and Dieter. It was one of the few times on the Camino I discussed spirituality in any depth, but I like to believe I helped Dieter on his interior spiritual journey. He helped me to organise my own thoughts into a coherent explanation. Pilgrims are generous to each other. Gaëlle could have taken her antiseptic home but she left it for me or others to use. I was reminded of the words of the Servant Song:

We are pilgrims on the journey
We are brothers on the road
We are here to help each other
Walk the mile and bear the load.

7. La joie n'est pas dans les choses, elle est en nous

(Joy is not in things, it is in us)

The earth had cooled down overnight and Saturday morning was overcast. As I moved out of Estaing into the countryside, I walked along the river. On one side the houses fringed the water and, on the other, townsfolk were hunting birds off their vegetable gardens. I reviewed my situation. I had covered the first 200 kilometres safely. I was proud of that achievement, as an old bloke not far off his eightieth birthday. Would I have done any better if, say, I tackled the Camino ten, twenty, thirty or forty years earlier?

So far I'd crossed the rugged countryside of the Auvergne and Massif Central, through picturesque towns and past roadside crosses, chapels, and gaunt roofless fortresses that marked the way for the faithful in centuries past. I followed in the footprints of pilgrims who, for over a thousand years, travelled through France on their way to the shrine of Saint James in Spain. I felt an affinity with the millions who had passed this spot, in the same way with those who would see my footprints as they followed me. I was part of a brotherhood stretching into the centuries.

My destination for the day was Conques. Conques is an important point on the way to Santiago. Many walkers who started at Le Puy were due to finish at Conques as the weekend was the last of the school holidays.

On the way as I paused at the village of Espeyrac, I found the church of Saint Pierre and lit two candles. Shortly I came to Sénergues and once again lit candles in the church of Saint Martin. Again I had the opportunity to light candles at a wayside chapel at Saint Marcel.

I always enjoyed the ritual of striking a match against the box and watching the flame breathe into the lifeless wick. The lit candle dispels the darkness. I liked to watch the candle burn. Sometimes the flame danced in the gentle breezes that may have flowed through the church. I thought of Maris and Joe. The two candles were symbols of their lives, but they were also symbols of the enlightenment I was seeking.

I passed through rugged country. Thick forest covered the hillsides and gorges. I never ceased to admire the wild beauty of creation. I was beginning to love the French countryside, giving it my full attention, holding it in the palm of my hand, as it were, treasuring it as precious. The pauses to rest after climbing a hill were awesome opportunities to look around at the clouds tumbling across the sky and the dense forest below, to see the birds soaring above the trees and admire the light and shade of the sun playing on the leaves.

The sun itself is a wonderful symbol, the source of all life on the planet. Caring for the natural world is a spiritual mission. We need to regard the environment with the eyes of the spirit and work towards its salvation. We are all in this together. If we don't regard the natural world as precious and sacred, our chances of saving the planet are doomed. I was travelling through two landscapes. The physical journey I was making through the back roads of France was in dialogue with an inner journey of the spirit.

Just before Conques I came across a panel in French, English and German:

Pilgrims and hikers, Sainte Foy (St Faith) welcomes you to Conques. This young (twelve years old) Christian martyr bore witness to her faith in Agen, where she was beheaded in AD 303. Her mortal remains arrived in Conques in 866 the reason why the abbey church was built.

With a sense of anticipation I followed the route around the hillside to Conques, which is nestled in a wild gorge and is one of the most beautiful villages of France with its narrow lanes and old, timber-frame houses. The abbey church of Sainte Foy is unique as it is the only medieval shrine on the Camino that survives intact. Founded in 819 in uninhabited forests, it provided isolation for prayer and meditation. Today, it is still a centre of spiritual refuge. As I looked down the hill to the abbey, I sensed I was in a special place.

I found my accommodation in the abbey at the rear of the church. *Accueil Abbaye Sainte Foy* is run by a community of Benedictine monks. The welcome was well organised with a team of greeters. Marguerite, a volunteer from Lyon, peeled off to look after me and showed me my dormitory up a wide circular staircase, the steps of which had been well worn by countless pilgrim feet.

The abbey had accommodation for ninety-six and by the end of the afternoon every bed was taken. I loved the medieval ambience of the abbey. Housed in the ancient building, it had been renovated with suitable fittings for the modern pilgrims. I enjoyed exploring the town, walking along its narrow lane-ways with their ancient buildings, souvenir shops, bars and restaurants. Conques is a tourist town and, being the weekend, there were plenty of strollers. I had time to admire the church.

In the tympanum over the front doors was a large carving of the Last Judgment. I could imagine the pilgrims of old crowding into the church, lying prostrate on the floor around the shrine of Sainte Foy so that there was hardly any room. The floor slopes to the front door to make it easier, according to my guidebook, to wash out the dirt left by the many tired feet. The old pilgrims rested and asked Sainte Foy for a safe passage to Santiago which might take up to a year of dangerous travel.

After dinner in the refractory everyone went to the church for prayers and a pilgrims' blessing. Being one of the few English speakers I was asked to read a prayer. The same prayer was then read in French, German and Dutch. The practice was to read the prayer in whatever languages were present.

I found the benediction moving. It was a sacred moment. After prayers and songs, the church was darkened and against the plain walls was projected a slideshow with the theme of darkness moving into the light.

My spirit stirred as I thought of the many candles I had lit along the Way. I felt as if I was in touch with a Presence. I had been blessed and fortified. I felt invigorated to continue, to put aside my anxieties and to accept that whatever came, God was on my side.

I was even tolerant of the snorers that night. Among my fellow roommates were at least six snorers who joined each other in harmony to sing a song of contentment.

Sunday was no day of rest; it was hard work, memorable for four vicious hills and taking the wrong turn twice. The first hill was outside Conques which had the pilgrim climbing 260 metres up the side of the wild gorge.

I was breathless and took judicious rests to look through crystal clear air to the view of Conques nestling between the wild gorges in the valley below. Then began a series of descents and ascents, the last climb to Livinhac-le-Haut the toughest. There will never be a time when a hill is not a challenge.

On the two wrong turns, both times I didn't get far before a local pointed out my error. The shells and red/white markers were less frequent so mistakes were easy enough to make. I loved those caring locals who wanted their vulnerable pilgrims on the right path. Perhaps they were pilgrims once themselves.

Because the day was so hard my progress was slow. I estimated I was walking about 2.5 kilometres per hour. I ignored any random reflections and just focused on the thought that each step was bringing me closer to my bed for the night. That thought egged me on and squeezed more effort out of my exhausted body.

I arrived at the *Gîte Communal* at 6.30 pm after tens hours of walking. I was hot, dirty and soaked in perspiration. I was thankful I made it. Among the guests were some friends from Conques. Marcel read the French at the benediction. I had seen Annie and Catherine a number of times over the last week. They came from Caen. I called them my gazelles because, although they spent plenty of time at rest, once they got going they moved fast. I shared a room with an older couple from Brittany. They had walked the Camino for several years, doing a week or so at a time. There were also two young men from Austria. They had already walked 1000 kilometres.

Together we sat down to dinner and became a family. I never ceased to be amazed at the welcome and instant camaraderie that is part of the Camino. This part of the pilgrim life is such a sharp contrast in this modern world where everywhere fear and mistrust of the stranger hold sway. That is everywhere except on the Camino. Suspicion is banished and the newcomer is presumed to be a friend and is a friend. The spirit of community that has reigned supreme down the centuries survives today.

I was always intrigued by the wayside graffiti, the spontaneous expression of pilgrims not long past.

Merci d'exister

(Thank you for being alive).

I could relate to that as I began every day with a prayer of thanks that I was alive and had the health, fitness and emotional strength to undertake such a difficult project.

La joie n'est pas dans les choses, elle est en nous

(Joy is not in things, it is in us)

was just along the wall. A more profound message followed:

Je me souviens que j'ai tout ce qu'il faut pour être bien ici et maintenant sauf si je laisse ma conscience perturbée par un passé qui est mort ou par un avenir imaginaire

(I remind myself that I have all I need to be happy here and now except if I allow my mind to be troubled by a dead past or an imagined future).

The author of that piece was Hubert. His message rang true for me. I had to remind myself to live in the present and not be too worried about the past or the future.

In 2006 I lived in Chambéry for three months. One Sunday at the cathedral I found a poem, *Vis le jour d'aujourdhui* (Live today today), the gist of which is that today (the present) is like a shaky footbridge and if you load it with yesterday's regrets or tomorrow's worries you'll overload it. It'll yield and you'll lose your foothold.

This day I arrived at Cajarc about 4.30 pm and found myself a bed at the *Gîte d'étape Le Pèlerin*. I visited the church of Saint Etienne for a pilgrims' blessing and lit two candles. The gîte did not offer dinner so I decided to cook a meal for myself rather than dine out.

At the supermarket I felt hungry and bought a couple of microwave dinners in case one wasn't enough. All the other guests went out to the local restaurant except for Dieter, the German with whom I had a long chat on that very hot night at Estaing. We greeted each other as old friends. We ate together. He referred to our earlier conversation and was keen to continue. We talked about people's motivation for undertaking the Camino. Dieter thought that God decided whether you walked the Camino or not because your health and strength were in His hands. I agreed with him, saying that, if you think you are in control, you're fooling yourself. I quoted Murphy's Law: *If anything is likely to go wrong, it will. If things haven't gone wrong yet, give 'em time.*

We were ready to settle into another long discussion when the lady whom I had seen singing in the church at La-Chaze-de-Peyre, who was knocked back at Les Gentianes, arrived late. She looked exhausted. Somehow they had squeezed her in. Anna was her name. She had no food and the supermarket was closed. I offered her my other microwave dinner and by the way she relished eating it, I'd say she was hungry. She called me Providence.

The spirit of the Camino is to share. What is given is given freely and what is received is received thankfully. The other guests arrived from their restaurant dinner and joined the three of us. The evening soon developed into a convivial gathering. We were an older group. By now the younger walkers were back at work and school, leaving the route for the retirees. We celebrated the eighty-first birthday of one of the walkers. Louis was a fit-looking wiry chap. It pleased me to realise I was not the oldest on the Camino.

In the morning I visited the supermarket and in one of the aisles I met Anna. She seemed to give me a special look as if she was looking inside of me. She followed me to the checkout and said quietly that she prayed for me that morning. I thanked her and said that pilgrims share and help each other out. That was the way of the Camino.

The day was warm but the country was flat and the walking was easy. What a change to the hills of earlier days. I walked steadily and effortlessly in a kind of weightless trance. The feeling was one of relief and luxury. I passed by two churches and lit candles in each. I was due to stay at Vaylats. The main accommodation was the *Monastère des Filles de Jesus* (Monastery of the Daughters of Jesus) but I chose the *Gîte Pèlerin Le Moulin* where an old mill had been renovated. In addition, a number of ramshackle buildings which reminded me of railway carriages housed toilets, bathroom, dining shelter and kitchen.

My host was Jacky. He was a former pilgrim, he told me, having walked the Camino in 2002. I'd doubt if he was up to walking today. He said he was diabetic. I wondered if he had other health problems. He was warm and welcoming and seemed pleased to see me. He was also expecting a couple but they didn't turn up, so I was the only guest.

Over the meal in a cluttered dining room with boots and utensils hanging from the ceiling the walls covered with tapestries and photos and arm chairs everywhere we shared our stories. Jacky had four children and seven grandchildren. He came originally from Toulouse and spent the winter there. He undertook the Camino and later opened his mill to pilgrims as a means of saying thank you. He was not in the business of running a *gîte* for the money.

I detected a note of melancholy in Jacky, as if he were living in the past and run down like the buildings in his *gîte*. We formed a bond, Jacky and I. He seemed a lonely old man and more than glad for my company. He produced a book and asked me to write a message. I noted that there were not many entries.

I slept on the ground floor of the mill while Jacky climbed the internal stairs to a room at the top. I thoroughly enjoyed staying with Jacky and sleeping in the mill. An enormous grinding wheel stood outside by the door and the inside was decorated with old utensils. I felt privileged as a welcome guest in his home.

In the morning he provided me with bread, cheese and a bottle of beer for lunch. Jacky embraced me as I left and I detected tears in his eyes. I shared his emotion. I was sad to leave him, realising I would never see him again. I would never see again others I had met, and had parted with them without emotion. Jacky meant more to me because I wondered if he was also saying goodbye to life in my person as I would have seemed to him vigorous and healthy. Could he see that his own life was deteriorating with bad health? As I made my way down the road, I consoled myself with the thought that my visit was like a lighted candle that for a moment banished the darkness from his life.

The walking was easy but the sky was overcast and rain began to fall. At first I had the route to myself but other walkers joined me later. I heard shooting all morning suggesting that the hunters were out in force. I came across an intriguing shrine. On two rocks someone had written *Solitude* on one and on the other *Larmes* (tears). On a bottle full of sand was written *Argent* (money). I wasn't sure what message the author was trying to convey.

I had thoughts of pushing on to Cahors, but I saw a rough sign pointed to *La Gîte Le pech* and decided that would do. Halfway up a steep hill leading to the *gîte*, I was met by a dog which turned and walked with me the remainder of the way. I felt he was shepherding me, as if he had come out to welcome me and lead me home. The dog's name I heard later was Jacques – fitting for his interest in pilgrims.

I arrived about 2.30 pm. The owners were absent but I found a woman sitting in the dining area. She told me she was ahead of her friends who were walking. She drove the car and took their baggage while they walked with day packs.

Eventually they arrived, six of them and later the eight of us sat down to a hearty dinner. A convivial night, everyone was French. It seemed to be a *let's be nasty to the English night* for there were lots of jokes told about them. I was the only English speaker but being an Australian who spoke French made me acceptable. During dinner rain began to fall steadily, which continued through the evening along with spectacular thunder and lightning. I passed into sleep to the sound of heavy rain drumming on the roof and windows. I hoped it would ease by morning.

Tuesday morning the rain was just as heavy. I debated whether I should take the day off, but I felt the urge to depart. I set off to a dark, dull grey morning on a cold, soggy day with all my wet weather gear in use. The rain continued all morning.

Eventually I was just as wet under my jacket as outside. Condensation and perspiration had the moisture running down my back. What was the point in wearing a jacket if you were just as wet underneath? Where there was dust the day before there was now mud and I felt as if half of France was sticking to my boots. I chastised myself for my restlessness, for not having the patience and good sense to remain at the dry *gîte* in comfort. I could hear my Maris calling me a dill.

By the time I reached Cahors the steady rain had turned into showers. Cahors is a large town surrounded by the river Lot on three sides. It was an important pilgrim stop and because it has a number of medieval buildings it could have been good for a rest day. I decided to push on, but not before visiting the cathedral (Saint Etienne's) and crossing the Pont Valentre reputed to be the finest fortified bridge in Europe. By the time I reached Les Mathieux the rain had ceased. I had booked into the *gîte Domaine des Mathieux*, which was also a *chambre et table d'hôtes*.

Although I had paid for the *gîte* I was given a room on my own. A large covered area outside my door allowed me to spread out my gear to dry. The outside of my pack was sopping wet but inside everything was in waterproof bags and was dry. My wet weather precautions had paid off.

I sat down to an excellent dinner with two other guests (man and wife) while the host and his wife joined us. The host was talkative but tended to ignore me and focus on the others. His monologue was about family issues and sounded like the older generation moaning about the excesses of the young.

Where have I heard that theme before?

8. May the road rise to meet you

I n the morning outside the *Les Mathieux gîte* I read a signpost – 350 kilometres back to Le Puy and 1153 to Santiago.

A few showers passed and although the track was thick with mud the way was relatively flat. I came across extensive fields of sunflowers. In the language of flowers, sunflowers represent faith, loyalty, happiness and optimism. For me they're a symbol of hope and life. They were planted in their millions in radioactive areas around Fukushima Nuclear Power Plant to soak up toxins from the ground left after the devastating tsunami of 2011. They were planted near Chernobyl after the 1986 nuclear accident for the same reason. They were used to symbolise nuclear disarmament in 1996 when Ukraine gave up it last warhead. The allure of this striking plant is reflected in Van Gogh's numerous attempts to capture its beauty.

I stopped for the night at Lascabanes. The *gîte* had a poetic name: *Le Nid des Anges* (Angels' Nest). It's housed in what was once the presbytery attached to the church. I was put in a room with four other men, all French. Philip used to work in Singapore, met many Australians and made regular trips to Australia. He said I was the first Australian whom he'd met who spoke French.

Before dinner a priest conducted a pilgrim's blessing and Mass in the adjacent church. This included his ritually washing our feet, a powerful metaphor. Jesus washed the feet of his disciples at the Last Supper. He was their servant, in the same way this priest was our servant washing the dust from our pilgrim feet. Washing the dirt can also be regarded as removing any imperfections that stand in the way of getting closer to God.

Fifteen sat down to dinner. There were familiar faces around the table, including the group I'd met at Le Pech. The conversation was lively, all in French, with many stories and jokes.

I hadn't used the internet for a while or sent an email. My family would be getting worried so I decided Thursday should be a short day, stopping at Montcuq about lunch time and using the internet during the afternoon. My guidebook had indicated that internet facilities were available. Once again the morning was showery but the good news was that there were no hills to speak of. I arrived at Montcuq late morning. It's a small hilltop town; the church dates back to the 12th century. Its name was the butt of one of the jokes over dinner the night before. It makes people smile because it's similar to the French vernacular for 'my arse'. I made my way to the *médiathèque* to use their computers only to find that it's closed on Thursdays. I was frustrated and annoyed. I was thinking that the joke was fitting and that Montcuq was an arse end of a town.

Montcuq was more or less halfway between Le Puy and Saint-Jean-Pied-de-Port. The village of Lauzerte came into view on top of a hill and it took some time to reach before beginning a steep ascent to the town, an ideal place for a walled city dating back to the 12th century. I found the *Gîte-Chambre-table d'hôtes Les Figuiers*. On the outside it looked rough as the building was being reclad but inside it was well fitted and welcoming. The hosts, Michel and Bernadette went out of their way to help their guests.

I read on a noticeboard that Mass was celebrated every

Friday at a *Maison de Retraite* (retirement home) at 4.30 pm. I asked Bernadette how I could get to the retirement home and she replied that she attended every Friday and I was welcome to come with her. So I was driven to Mass through this medieval town. The Mass was sad. The congregation consisted of very elderly people in various stages of decline. Many were in wheelchairs and cared for by attendants. I'm not sure how much they were aware of. I felt awkward but I did my best to say hello (*bon jour*) to them. The priest tried to deliver a homily but one lady began giggling and exclaimed over and over 'Il est fou!' (He's mad!). The priest was taken aback. The attendants scolded the old thing. I half expected one of them to slap her, but eventually she was wheeled out and the homily and the Mass continued.

Back at the *gîte* the meal was excellent. In fact, everything about this *gîte* was excellent. I even managed to check my emails. The dinner table saw a mixture of pilgrims and tourists. I was asked the usual questions. Why had I come all this way? Remembering my evening at Jacky's, I said to say thank you. How come I spoke French so well? I still did not believe I was that fluent. How old was I? I had to thank God for my health and fitness.

In the morning I left the *gîte* and walked to the main square, *la place des Cornières*, where I found a flourishing market in the process of being set up. I lingered over the stalls and bought bread and cheese for lunch. Walking through the town I appreciated the manner in which many medieval buildings had been preserved. I passed the *Maison de Retraite* where I had attended Mass the previous afternoon. Peering through the gate I admired the garden but remembered with sadness the life of the elderly who lived there. They were at the end of their lives, waiting to die, truly in God's waiting room. I wondered how long I had before I'd be on God's threshold. No time to ponder as I was back in the present, faced with a steep hill. I looked back to rest and admire the view of Lauzerte, an ideal location for a fortified town, a reminder of a past which knew many troubles and invasions.

Under a cloudless sky the greens and browns of the gentle rolling hills were more vibrant and simmering in the brilliant sun. I was in the midst of rich farming land, a land of vineyards and orchards. One of the great aspects of the French countryside is the number of chapels you pass. Most of them are open. I passed Saint Sernin. The inside was unfurnished apart from a kneeler, but on one of the walls was a set of photographs and description of how the chapel was restored. It was a welcome place to pause and to be refreshed with the spirit of the people whose church this was. Outside was a cemetery and I enjoyed reading the inscriptions. I passed a small wayside stall which was unattended but offered melons, grapes and tomatoes. There were many stalls on the way offering the season's produce. Some were free, others had a money tin to accept what the purchaser was inclined to give. I purchased some grapes.

I stopped for the night at La Baysse where I had made a reservation at the *gîte/chambre d'hôtes*. The *gîte* part was a caravan at the back while *chambre d'hôtes* guests were in the house. In all there were four guests. A couple stayed in the *chambre d'hôtes* while Bernard shared the caravan with me.

Bernard worked in Paris as a senior executive with a multinational telecommunications company with a subsidiary in Australia. He had taken a few days off work to walk and to think. He told me that that was often his practice when he had a problem to resolve. He did not tell me his problem. However, he mentioned he had two colleagues who were Australian.

Neither of them spoke French, nor had they taken the trouble to learn. He described them as lazy, and contrasted them with me who did not live in France but spoke good French. He would tell them about me when he returned to work. Bernard spoke good English himself but he chose to speak in French. He tested me for we discussed some complex subjects. In my corporate days as a management consultant the Australian subsidiary of Bernard's company had been one of my clients. He seemed thoughtful and caring and I imagined him a capable and honest executive. We exchanged cards. He suggested that when I arrived in Paris I should ring him. I was gratified that he wanted to continue our brief contact.

We dined on the terrace on a warm clear evening. Our host and his wife joined us. The meal was excellent and the produce, our hosts said, was grown on their land. We had a quiet and intimate dinner, the six of us. In the distance our hosts pointed out a shadow on the horizon which he said was the Pyrenees, still hundreds of kilometres away. I was making my way slowly and gently across France.

I decided to stop at Moissac, which was only twelve kilometres away. I arrived to find a large flourishing market. Stalls occupied all the streets. They sold everything. I had plenty of time to inspect the stalls and to visit the major sites. Moissac is a large town. It's been a major pilgrim halt from the middle ages onwards. I visited the abbey church of Saint-Pierre, a former Benedictine monastery founded in the 7th century with impressive cloisters. The abbey was first built in the 11th century. There was plenty to see, capitals full of Bible stories and lives of the saints. Being a Sunday, I jostled with crowds of tourists and visitors. I was happy to quit the centre of town to find my accommodation for the night.

The *gîte d'étape Ultreia* was on the way out of town opposite the railway station. There seemed to be plenty of trains although none of them stopped. I found my host in his garden along with his two-year-old son Mathiew digging up potatoes. I shook hands with young Mathiew. His father said that I was the first guest whom he allowed to shake his hand. I replied that perhaps my experience with six grandchildren helped me to gain Mathiew's trust. Rom and Aiden were Irish.

My night with them stands out because of their warm welcome. I felt part of their family. It was quaint to hear the Irish accent. Aiden spoke French perfectly but you could hear the distinctive Irish accent in Rom's French. They told me some great stories of their battles with the French bureaucracy to obtain the necessary permits for their *gîte*. Rom wore a t-shirt describing the weather in Ireland. Under a heading, *The Four Seasons*, were four drawings of the same cartoon character in Summer, Autumn, Winter and Spring being drenched by rain. Rom had a wonderful sense of humour. He handled the anxious French guests' queries well and joked with me that he was leading me into temptation in offering me a beer. I replied that although I was abstaining from sex on the Camino, I was not abstaining from alcohol.

I mentioned to Rom that I had read a strong recommendation of his *gîte* on a blog site, written by a former guest. He replied, 'That would be Margaret.' She was a New Zealander, had stayed two years previously and had set up a network of former pilgrims. He asked me for her blog address so that he could look it up himself. I asked him why he and his wife, an Irish couple, had taken the business of running a *gîte* in France. He replied that the two of them had walked the Camino and had grown to love it. They hoped to walk in Spain later in the year, with their two-year-old son, when their *gîte* was closed for the winter.

We dined at a long table stretching the length of the garden in the softly lit twilight, a memorable night full of jokes and chatter. At the end of the meal Rom handed out souvenir cards. The Irish Blessing was in English, French and German. The Irish Blessing is one of my favourites. It greets visitors to my home on a clay plaque by the front door.

May the road rise to meet you
May the wind be always at your back
May the sun shine warm upon your face
The rains fall soft upon your fields and
Until we meet again may God hold you in the palm of his hand.

I shared a room with two Irish ladies, two sisters, who happened to arrive on the one train that stopped. They had no idea that their hosts would be fellow countrymen. They were planning to walk for a week and spend the time catching up as they lived in different parts of Ireland. It was a nice relaxation to chat quietly in English. Instead of the usual questions, one of them asked if I was a churchgoer. When I replied yes she said that she no longer attended church. Because of the scandals about paedophile priests and cover-up by the church, Irish Catholics were disillusioned. They were still seeking the Divine but not through the structure of the church. I did not need to ask why she was doing the Camino. Although they had given up on institutional religion they were still seeking a spirituality to live by.

Rom reminded me of a father seeing off his children as he said good bye to his guests in the morning. When I made a comment, he replied that while the guests were with him, they were his family, except that after they walked out his door he never saw or heard of them again.

A sign outside on the wall pointed the way to St Jacques, 1085 kilometres away.

The day turned out to be one of the easiest so far as the route followed a canal towpath in the shade of large trees at first near the river Tarn and later Garonne. It was a delight to see the occasional boat or barge pass by. So calm and tranquil! I kept meeting and passing the Irish sisters. The route crossed over a bridge to the other side until it left the canal and struck out into the open. Then followed some steep climbing but I made Auvillar in good time. I stayed in the *Gîte Communal*, a former presbytery. Auvillar is a small hilltop town with a medieval market hall where they used to measure grain, well restored, in an arcaded square.

Being Monday, all the shops were shut but I found a small restaurant, and while eating my meal in the courtyard amused myself by watching a cat playing with a mouse at my feet. Eventually the mouse escaped. What would our Australian health authorities have to say! Here in this medieval town it seemed so natural and part of creation. That's what cats do – play with mice.

The following morning I passed through orchards where the fig and peach trees were loaded with fruit. I passed by fields of sunflowers, always an uplifting experience. My contact with the natural world was liberating and keeping me free to stay with the present. The brilliant day was proclaiming that I was in and part of God's creation. The previous evening in my *Guide Spirituel du Pèlerin* I read Saint Francis of Assisi's *Canticle of the Sun*. Also known as the *Canticle of Creatures*, it sings of the praise given to God through all the creatures, through Brother Sun, Sister Moon and the Stars, Brothers Wind and Air, clouds and storms and all the weather, Sister Water, Brother Fire and Sister Mother Earth. All creatures live under the same Brother

Sun and walk on the same Mother Earth. Just through their existence they are honouring a higher power. My existence, too, is honouring a higher presence.

The next day was Wednesday the 15th September. I had one month before I flew back to Australia on 15th October. Everyone was walking westwards, but for the first time I encountered a pilgrim walking in the opposite direction. Joseph said he was Spanish and his tiny wife was Portuguese. He wore an enormous pack with the label *Santiago a Roma* and his wife was equally dominated by her pack. He said he had lost his job and his house in the global financial crisis and had decided to walk to Rome where he hoped to meet the Pope. He spoke good English and was very charming. He could have been a conman or he could have been genuine but he was definitely one of the brotherhood, a Camino character. He said he had no money and offered to sell me some beads which his wife had made so I bought a small necklace. I wondered if I was meeting Jesus. I had a joke with my fellow parishioners before I left that as I was undertaking a spiritual journey I might meet Jesus just as the disciples met Jesus on the road to Damascus. If Joseph was Jesus, he was in heavy disguise. My conscience was clear. I had helped Joseph on the way to Rome by pausing to encourage him and by buying his beads.

I stopped at Marsalan in a combined *gîte/chambre d'hôtes*. *L'enclos du Tabus*. The gîte was in cabins down the back where I shared a cabin with three ladies. Lucy, Millicent and Anna were walking for two weeks. They, too, had met Joseph and bought his beads. The next morning was overcast and showery. My three cabin mates were aiming for Condom and, because of limited time, were taking a shorter route which by passed Le Romieu.

My hosts at the dinner table suggested that Le Romieu was well worth a visit and somehow intuitively I knew that for me their advice was right. On the way to Le Romieu I passed through a dense dark forest of tall trees. I was impressed by the number of hides in the tree tops and the long precarious ladders for access although I'm not sure if the hides were for bird watchers or for hunters. In this wilderness I met a group of about fifty elderly who were out for an excursion perhaps bird watching. They recognised me as a pilgrim and wished me '*Bon Chemin.*'

The village of Le Romieu takes its name from the *romieux* (pilgrims) who passed through it on the way to Santiago. It has an enormous church for its size, an indication of its former importance. The 14th century *Saint Pierre Collégiale* was built by Clement V, one of the Avignon Popes. Under a grey sky and an occasional drizzle, I visited the *Collégiale* and walked around the extensive cloisters and garden, climbed one of the two towers of the church and admired the extensive view of the green countryside stretching out to the horizon. Along the Camino the pilgrim sees many crosses, religious icons, images of Saint James and other saints, as well as many churches and chapels, all reminders of the influence of the Catholic Church, but Le Romieu stands out in my mind because this influence can be witnessed in one concentrated spot. It's a compact heap of architectural splendour built for the glory of an earlier age. The entire site is recognised as World Heritage by UNESCO.

I'm glad I took the trouble to visit Le Romieu. In the messiness of our modern life we sometimes forget that history is part of our existence. Along the Camino I was reminded constantly that there is a past as well as a present, that the past has very much to do with the present. If I had taken the shorter route to Condom, I might have missed out on an important lesson, or rather, a reminder that the experience of the journey itself, more than the journey is the goal. Once again, I was filled with a sense of awe at the world around me.

9. Vivre le chemin

(Live the way)

I passed by the chapel of Sainte Germain. I lit two candles. I prayed for my sister Maria and wondered how she was coping with Joe gone. I looked at a display of photographs on the chapel's restoration. What does it take for a disused chapel to be renovated and restored? I imagined the love that had been poured into the work. I had come across a number of these chapels, no doubt former places of sanctuary. They seemed to be in the middle of nowhere, yet there were signs that they were well cared for. They were open, clean and often had fresh flowers. Someone unseen loved them.

The landscape was open and in the distance I could see Condom, like a smudge on the horizon. I arrived there about 11.30 in good time to look over the shops and the large cathedral of Saint Pierre. Condom is a town of about 8000 people, the centre of the Armagnac industry. The liqueur is exported around the world. Its medieval buildings attracted many tourists but I didn't bother to hang around. Back in the open country, I detoured to Larressingle, a tiny fortified town, completely walled, the fortress of the Bishop of Condom in the middle ages. How the past races to meet the present!

A short distance beyond Larressingle lay the *Gîte-la Ferme de Tollet*, about a kilometre off the main route. The track was narrow and almost overgrown but I pushed my way through to the farm gate where I crossed an enclosure with a rather solemn horse eyeing the intruder. A note on the building door told me to make myself at home. I found a lounge and kitchen as well as three bedrooms. It turned out I was in the wrong building. I was in the *chambre d'hôtes* rather than the *gîte* which was attached to the main farm house, a little further down the hill. However it didn't matter. I enjoyed being on my own. In the lounge was a small library. I picked up a book on *La Corrida* (bullfighting). Lavishly illustrated with colour photography it described in detail the art of bullfighting. The author was a passionate enthusiast and although he mentioned the controversy surrounding the sport, he justified it on the basis of its tradition of disciplined training and preparation.

On the walls were some certificates of attainment for *La Corrida*. The recipient had the same surname as the owner of the farm. I joined the farmer's family for dinner, made from the farm's produce. I was the only guest. The family was the farmer, his wife and four-year-old daughter. An old man sat in a chair away from the table. I guessed he was one of their parents and suffered dementia. The wife led the old chap to another room and after dinner she and her daughter disappeared. The farmer and I continued to chat. The recipient of the certificates was his uncle. I was in bullfighting country and many of the surrounding towns had their festivals.

The evening was enriching. I was accepted into the family. Being a pilgrim does have its rough patches but the great benefit is your interaction with the people. If you were a tourist in a vehicle you would drive by and see the sites but you are in an insulated capsule. As a pilgrim you are vulnerable and to some extent helpless and you have to rely on the local people. My host also made Armagnac and a cherry liqueur. We had a drink or two after dinner. In fact, we finished the cherry liqueur, so I was heady as I staggered up the hill to my bed.

In the morning I pushed my way up the overgrown track to the main route. Not long after I arrived at the Pont d'Artigues.

A notice indicating I was at a World Heritage site described the bridge as one of the oldest pilgrim bridges still in existence. There was also a notice with a map of all the churches along the Via Podiensis, the name of the route from Le Puy to Saint-Jean-Pied-de-Port. At first, crosses were erected at crossroads to mark the way, and churches and chapels were added followed by hospital and monasteries. Shortly after the bridge was one of these small chapels. The *Eglise des Routges* is one of the oldest churches in the district.

My guidebook mentioned the small door on the side of the church. This was the entrance used by the Cagots. They were an outcast population, found mainly in the south west of France. They lived segregated lives. They were regarded as unclean, leprous, syphilitic and bearers of all types of evil. As a consequence they were not allowed to enter churches by the main door but had to use a special side entrance. They were not even allowed to be buried in the cemeteries that the rest of the population used.

Poor bastards, I thought, as I tried the door. I imagined a Cagot entering to be met by the hostile gaze of the other 'Christians'. Every age and culture has its outcasts, its pariahs, its untouchables. The situation with the Cagots was poignant in that they lived in a Christian community. Christians are supposed to be followers of Christ who accepted everyone, particularly those who lived on the margins.

Up to now I had a nagging discomfort in my back each afternoon but today the muscles on the lower left side were painful. My back was handling the pack weight in the morning but after the lunch break fatigue set in and the pack became heavier and weighed me down.

I was relieved to stop for the night at Manciet where I stayed at *Gîte Chez Mathieu.* The other guests were Catherine, a French lady and Anita, a Canadian from British Columbia who had lived in Europe most of her life. Mathieu was away for the weekend playing rugby so his sister looked after us. I tried to stay in *gîtes* in quiet rural locations, but this one was on a busy highway. The noisy traffic passed all night. In the morning the toilet was not flushing, which reduced the ladies to a panic. Assuming that the workings of French toilets were no different from Australian, I removed the top and fixed the problem. The ladies were grateful, commenting that it was good to have a man around. It was nice to feel useful.

After the pain of the previous afternoon I decided to listen to my body, which was telling me it needed an easy day. I left the gîte at 9.00 am, the last to depart. The day was overcast. I stopped at Lelin Lapujelle for lunch. The village provided a pleasant picnic spot complete with tables so I ate my lunch with a group of French walkers. They were interested in my coming from Australia and asked the usual questions. Adjacent to the picnic park was a small one-roomed school. I enjoyed listening to the busy hum coming from the open window. It was nice to think that this village had enough children to support a school, particularly as I had passed others which were closed.

In the midst of history about people long dead, it reminded me of the present moment and of life being lived right now. I hoped the village was proud of its little school. I would have loved to talk to the teacher. I recalled my own experience. At the age of twenty, I was sent to a remote one teacher school in a tiny community in the Victorian Mallee. The people had to fight hard to keep their little school open. I had happy memories of the family atmosphere and the trust the children had in their teacher. Sometimes the children called me 'Dad', and the little ones took my hand.

A broken sign on the side of the GR65 indicated that the *Gîte Dubarry* was 300 metres off the track. The *gîte* was as ramshackle as the sign. The buildings looked centuries old. Some parts had fallen down. Farm machinery and rusty equipment were lying around. The exterior was not inviting but the interior had been refurbished and was spacious and welcoming. The kitchen looked brand new. The warmth, friendliness and welcome of my host Pierre made this a memorable *gîte*. I met his wife Veronique and their twelve-year-old son Jean-Charles who was as charming as his father and used to speaking with adults. Jean-Charles was yet a child and I saw him playing with his little cars in a sandpit. Two fine looking black Labradors came running out to meet me and hung around. I commented how fine they looked. Pierre said they were strays whom someone had abandoned. He would have to get rid of them although by the way his son fondled and played with them he would have some resistance.

The other guests were a couple from Quebec – Claude and Martha. I had to listen carefully to their French. I'm told that many French have difficulty understanding their Quebecois brothers. Pierre joined us for dinner. He enjoyed his role of playing host. It was great to feel part of his family. By staying at a small *gîte* attached to a farm you get to know the people, a chance which the average tourist staying at a hotel would never get. Pierre could have been an Aussie farmer for his laid back manner. He was planning to renovate and rebuild his *gîte*, he said, but he was taking his time as he had a working farm to run.

In the morning I departed at the same time as Jean-Charles left on his bike for school. The countryside was flat and foggy so there was not much to see until I reached Barcelone du-Gers where I rang my sister Maria to wish her a happy birthday.

Although my back ached I made good time and about 2.00 pm crossed the bridge over the river Adour into Aire-sur-l'Adour, an ancient town with a population of over 6000.

I walked through the town and up a hill to the *Gîte d'étape privé Hospitalet Saint-Jacques* and after my usual routine, I went back to the town and found an internet site with the best facilities on the Camino. Eight computers were available and by the size of the crowd the locals made good use of them. What a contrast to Montcuq, my arse end town, where the facilities were closed the day I arrived.

I waited my turn and was able to read and send emails back home. I had a mailing list of family and friends and a number had been tracking me with their maps of the towns and villages I was passing through. It's nice to think that I had a group of fans back home.

I bought a few items at the supermarket to prepare my dinner but back at the *gîte* everyone pooled their food for a communal dinner. There were eight guests. I chatted with two Czech girls and Xavier, a young Frenchman. The hosts, Odile and André were exceptional. They were pilgrims themselves having walked the Camino several times. André looked after people's feet, gave them massages and treated blisters. He and Odile were keen to give as much information as possible. They shared their lives with their pilgrims.

10. Vis le jour d'aujourdhui

(Live today today)

Thursday 23rd September. That day I came across the first of the notices from *l'alchemiste*. Attached to a tree on a slate board was his message:

Accepte l'inévitable.

I thought of my aching back. Through all the twists and turns and killer hills the Camino had found my weakness. I thought I was strong enough in both body and mind to withstand its rigours but the Camino had brought me down from my smug pedestal. I had to accept that my back would continue to cause me discomfort. If it was my only physical problems in my thirty-eight days to date on the road, I had done well, in contrast to many blistered feet and the suffering of their owners. I had about a week to go and was aiming to take it as leisurely as possible. No heroic stunts or pushing myself. Just take things gently. *Il faut marcher doucement.*

Throughout the day I continued to meet my friends of the road. Claude and Martha, my French Canadians had stayed in another *gîte* in Aire sur l'Adour. Xavier, the young Frenchman from the previous night, was clutching his rosary beads as he walked. I came across the two Czech ladies. We all came together at the communal *gîte* at Miramont Sensacq, which was run by volunteers from the *Landes Jacquarian* group. Jacquarians are friends of Saint Jacques. They have a special devotion to the saint, run various *gîtes* on behalf of the owners, usually the local town council, and sometimes produce guides to help the pilgrims on their way. I was interviewed and welcomed by Georges. The *gîte* accommodated about twenty guests. Four of us, including Xavier still clutching his rosary beads, found the local church for a Mass in the late afternoon.

After Mass the priest invited us to his house and offered us a drink of the local liqueur. He was a jovial extravert who talked about the local community and his attitudes towards the institutional church, which weren't flattering. Back at the *gîte* everyone – including the volunteers – joined together for a communal meal.

The surge of conversation around the tables reminded me of bubbling water. Some of the pilgrims had lost their sense of time. One young man sitting opposite had deliberately left his watch at home. He did not know what day it was. I was envious of his ability to surrender himself to the day, to the moment. I told him about my poem *Vis le jour d'aujourdhui* (Live today today). I'm always reminding myself that I should but I seem to be thinking ahead all the time. An Austrian girl also wasn't wearing a watch. She had a definitely lost look about her and I hoped she was able to look after herself. Next to me Yvette, one of the volunteers, told me her life story, starting from when she was abandoned as a child during the war. She struck me as a needy person and, if I had offered to go to bed with her, she might have accepted. The priest turned up during the dinner to say g'day. Georges told him of the various countries present but he interrupted Georges saying he already knew the Australian.

The evening was memorable because everyone lingered over the dinner and then everyone pitched in to help with the clean-up. We had become a family where everyone had the time to talk to each other in contrast to the fears of modern society where people seem too suspicious and have forgotten the art of sharing and communication. I shared a room with four mature French ladies. I imagined they would have been beautiful in their youth and stirred the hearts of all the young men. Now their beauty was in its twilight but they would have looked elegant dressed up for a night at the theatre. They didn't look too bad to me in their hiking gear.

It rained during the night and was still raining when I left. It rained most of the day. At Sensacq I visited the church dating from the 11th century. At Pimbo the rain was heavier so I took shelter in the church where I ate my lunch in a corner at the back. A pilgrim popped his head in and gave me a second look as if I was doing something sacrilegious. Pimbo is one of the oldest fortified villages in the Landes. The church was built on the site of a monastery found by Charlemagne. In the afternoon I came across another message from *l'alchemiste*. On a slate nailed to a tree his advice was:

Tais-toi. Ecoute.

(Be quiet, Listen).

My back was aching when I arrived at Arzacq Arraziguet, grateful for the relief of removing my pack.

I was about to leave the department of Les Landes and into the Pyrennes-Atlantiques. I had already walked through several departments. I started at Haute-Loire and then walked through Lozere, Aveyron, Lot, Tarn et Garonne, Gers and Landes. I was also on the border of France and Bearn which was once a separate country. The area reeked of history. From its origins in Roman days, it had progressed through an era when it had been taken over by various noble families including the kings of Navarre. It became part of France in 1620. During the Napoleonic wars Wellington's army swaggered through here. In the meantime the humble pilgrim plodded through the region on his way to Santiago. How many made it in medieval times is not recorded except that it was a hazardous journey with no guarantees of returning home. Today's pilgrim's chances of returning home are high although I came across memorials to pilgrims who had died on route – gentle reminders of our mortality.

I stayed in the *gîte d'étape communal* where I shared a room with the pilgrim who gave me the evil eye in the church at Pimbo. He was a severe man of few words and talked to no one. He went to bed early and buried his head under the pillow. He was not on the Camino to talk to his fellow pilgrims. Audrey was from Switzerland. She was chatty. She was to commence walking the following day and showed her apprehension by asking many questions. The other roommate was Roger. He asked me the usual questions. Thirty people sat down to dinner. Among them were many of my friends from the road. Claude and Martha greeted me warmly as if I had known them for years. Many of the people from the previous night including the ladies with whom I shared the room were among the diners. Once again, the magic of the Camino brought this diverse mob together in instant camaraderie.

Shortly after leaving Arzacq Arraziguet I came across the Pilgrim Tree. *L'Arbre du Pèlerin* was decorated with many emblems – shells, old boots, horse shoes, a walking stick, statues of Saint Jacques and the Virgin, rosary beads, crosses, flags, artificial flowers. A small sign read:

Chemin des Etoiles

(Way of the stars)

L'alchemiste had been at work. On his slate he had written, *Avoir l'audace d'y croire et le courage de faire* (Have the daring to believe and the courage to act). Shortly along the way *l'alchemiste* had been at work again: *Ce que tu AS est suffisant pour ETRE – plus.* (What you have is enough to be – more).

Having moved into the department of Pyrenees-Atlantiques I had to accept I had left the flat country behind. I started climbing hills. By way of compensation the views were great and in the distance I could sight the Pyrenees. I continued to meet old friends. Claude and Martha said goodbye as they were keen to push ahead to meet a flight schedule. I met some of the people from Miramont Sansacq including Xavier, still holding his rosary beads.

I was pleased to arrive at Uzan as my back was aching on the lower left side. The *gîte* was a house in its own grounds and the owner lived opposite. I was the first to arrive and I settled into a room with one bed. While I was resting, a donkey brayed outside my window. Five others arrived, two couples and one bloke. The man was Swiss-German, one couple was French and the other was from Quebec. In sharp contrast to so many evenings on the Camino no one was friendly, a reminder of the real world. My efforts to reach out failed. The couples kept to themselves and the man was the silent type. No one was interested in talking to a lonely old Australian. I'd been on my own other nights when I was able to provide for myself sufficient company, but this time I felt isolated, estranged, discontent, as if something was missing. I was on the other side of the world from home, far away from family and friends.

The evening had its compensation. There were no shops in the village but the owner offered farm produce for sale, so I bought some eggs, tomatoes and bread. I have to say that those tomatoes were among the most delicious I have ever tasted. I have often joked about the search for a decent tomato because the supermarket variety is so often tasteless, but I can say I found the perfect tomato in a tiny village in the southwest of France.

I left the *gîte* Sunday morning and commenced walking. I had now walked for forty days, a distance of about 650 kilometres. I had answered the call of the Camino. I had found a routine and settled into the rhythm of the days. I had to admit I was looking forward to the end of the week by which time I would have reached Saint-Jean-Pied-de-Port. I had almost achieved what I had set out to do this year. I aimed to finish at Saint Jean and then return to continue the journey to Santiago. Right at that moment I was ready to go home.

I soon came upon the village of Geus-d'Arzacq, a clean neat village with a modern church. I sat in the church and contemplated. What had I found out about myself? I gazed at the two candles I'd just lit. *I'm walking for you, Maris,* I said to myself, but also for something more. When I began walking I was preoccupied with whether I had the strength to persevere but, as I moved through France, I felt a deep affinity with the countryside. In my inner journey I recognised and respected the value of my interconnectedness and interdependence with all people, all living creatures and all creation. I knew this intellectually but now I was feeling it with my heart. It's as if I was walking with God. The God that I knew in church was perhaps a small god but here on the Camino I was glimpsing an unknowable mystery. When I attempted to speak about God, I had to remind myself that I couldn't describe God. I could only use images and thoughts that grasped at insights which built up an idea of what God was like. My idea, however, is not what God actually is. No matter, I felt that God was with and within me. When I spoke to God, I spoke to a Presence deep within me. Some people called this presence their Higher Self. I found myself continually expressing thanks to be part of God's creation. As I set off each morning I was deeply grateful for the fact that I was alive, that I had the fitness and health for this caper when so many of my age were suffering from illness. I came upon another message from *l'alchemiste* which told me who he was. He ran a *gîte d'étape* at Navarreux and offered the pilgrim the opportunity to *vivre le chemin (live the way)*. I reached Arthez de Bearn in good time and found my *gîte* on the edge of town. The *gîte-Boulangerie Brousse* appeared run down from the outside and although inside was comfortable enough I didn't like the feel of it. There was no host to greet us. The guests settled in themselves, all men.

My roommate was Georges from Switzerland. No meal was served at the *gîte* and being Sunday all the restaurants were closed. However, one at the other end of town opened after 8.00 pm for pilgrims only. At the appointed time we walked the length of the town, a long drawn out affair shaped like a banana which followed the ridge.

Nine of us from seven countries sat down to dinner, the nationalities being Danish, Swiss, Austrian, Canadian, German, French and Australian. I gained a new appreciation of the world as one community. In such a cosmopolitan group I enjoyed an evening which made up for the loneliness of the previous evening and the pain and discomfort of the day.

The evenings over dinner were always opportunities to get to know each other. You fell into company so easily and the conversation and storytelling were invigorating. I was always grateful that I had the desire and the skills to communicate with my fellow pilgrims. I could speak English, passable French and a smattering of German. Perhaps it would not have mattered if I could only speak English. Our Danish pilgrim only knew Danish and a smattering of German and English but he nevertheless communicated and enjoyed himself.

We were late leaving and a noisy lot going home. We had nearly two kilometres to walk back to the *gîte*, a blessing in disguise and a chance to clear the head after the copious amounts of red wine the restaurateur had supplied to this mob of internationals who had drunk themselves into a mutli-lingual haze.

After such a heavy night, the morning was refreshingly cool as we walked to the *boulangerie* for breakfast. The *gîte* was owned by the *boulanger*, hence its name. It was snug sitting at the table surrounded by the ovens and the delicious smell of freshly baked bread. For the most part the walking was flat although two steep hills of the killer variety relieved the monotony. *L'alchemiste* had three messages today. Two were repeats. One reminded the passer-by of his *gîte* at Navarreux, the second reminded us that what you have already is sufficient for you to live. The third message was new:

Tu es ton bien le plus precieux

(You are your most precious possession)

I liked that.

As I walked along a shaded path by a river I noticed a bicycle propped against a tree. I couldn't see the rider but a few metres ahead an older man with a fishing rod emerged out of the bushes. He was very friendly and ready for a chat as if he hadn't talked to anyone for ages and craved company. He told me his name was Joseph. He spoke in French but lacked fluency as if it wasn't his first language. He told me he had been born in the area and spoke the local language (Béarnaise?). He had lived here all the life with the exception of the war when he was sent to Germany as a forced worker. He told me his philosophy of life which was essentially an appreciation of the family. He recommended I should visit the sanctuary of Notre Dame de Muret. He said it was a magical place and, after intercession, miracles had occurred. I admired the conviction of his belief. I tried to leave him but he always had something more to say. Perhaps I was meeting Jesus, I thought, so I should stay and hear him out. I was saved by another pilgrim. The Dane from the previous night arrived so Joseph turned his attention to him, although, as the Dane had no French, I didn't imagine he'd get much of a hearing.

The turn off to the shrine was just up the hill and, after receiving such a strong recommendation, I had to look. I found the sanctuary in an open area on the top of the hill. I stayed awhile to absorb the 'magic' of the place. I could appreciate how pilgrims valued the sanctuary with its images of the Virgin and were prompted to pray. The sanctuary looked over the surrounding countryside although the view on one side of one of France's largest natural gas plants, a bizarre piece of the industrial world, dominated the rural landscape.

At La Sauvelade an impressive abbey church is all that remains of the monastery founded in the 12th century. I stayed in the *gîte Le P'tit Laa* which was also a café, restaurant, small grocery and a pizza parlour. The young woman running the café welcomed me into the *gîte*, although I gained the impression she was not to be messed with. She had strict rules about leaving packs and boots outside, etc., gave me the rundown in French and to make sure I got the message also in English. I came to admire this lady for her many skills. She had three children under six, but also ran the café and restaurant and kept her pilgrims in order. Her husband was the cook. We enjoyed his dinner in the restaurant and in the meantime she helped the children with reading and drawing and he made pizzas for the locals.

Shortly after Sauvelade I read final messages from the *l'alchemiste*. The first one said:

L'obstacle t'est proposé pour que tu le dépasses

(The obstacle is put to you to overcome)

Just along the track was his second. This time his slate board was broken and was partly on the ground. Putting the pieces together gave the message:

Ce que est très très dur rend très très fort

(What is very very hard makes one very very strong)

I enjoyed reading his motivational one-liners. They struck me as clever marketing. There were many advertisements along the way for *gîtes*, but *l'alchemiste* had the passer-by intrigued. At least he intrigued me. He had packed a lot of wisdom into notices that had the potential to inspire.

I was now in Basque country (Pays Basque), all the signs being in French and Basque. I arrived at Navarrenx about 2.00 pm and met the Canadian from the previous night. He told me he was staying *chez l'alchemiste* and that it looked very good. I was curious to see what kind of *gîte l'alchemiste* ran. I had already reserved a bed at the communal *gîte* but before checking in I tried my luck with *l'alchemiste*. I found him, a large man in early middle age, in his *gîte* cooking the evening's dinner. Alas, the *gîte* was full (*complet*) for the night. He seemed disappointed that he could not help me and offered a bed for the next night. I was disappointed, too. The *gîte* looked exotic. There was a display of crystals and a notice indicating he conducted meditation sessions. Staying here could have been another experience. I was intrigued by the name he gave himself. Alchemy was the medieval science which sought to turn baser metals into gold and to find an elixir of life. The name suggests transformation. Staying at his *gîte* provided an opportunity for change? Or was it referring to the Camino's potential to transform?

'Almost everyone who has walked the Way of Saint James,' says one of my guidebooks, *'would probably agree that it has changed their lives in some way.'*

I found the communal *gîte* sterile in comparison. The evening had no camaraderie over dinner for I cooked a meal on my own in the *gîte's* kitchen. The good news was sharing a room with three ladies from New Brunswick. Mary, Sally and Jo were retired teachers. By now most of the walkers were retired, possibly the major group who had the time to commit themselves in this fast moving 21st century to the slow pace of long distance walking. It was a pleasant change to speak English with one's roommates.

The town's history emerged out of the cool morning as I walked downhill alongside ramparts erected in the 16th century. Up to now the Pyrenees had been like a shadow on the horizon but I gained my first clear view of a series of peaks and hills that seem to repeat themselves into the distance, a definite indication that I was nearing the end of my journey. I was sad yet I was happy to finish. I had been on the track for forty-five days and covered over 700 kilometres. Walking each day, finding a place to sleep and eat had become the simple daily routine. I had reduced my life to the basics. My major tasks were survival, self-care, ensuring that my feet and legs were sound, showering and hand washing my clothes. I was keeping life simple. I had become part of the Camino and the Camino had become part of me.

I reckoned that by the time I reached Aroue I had about forty-eight kilometres to Saint-Jean-Pied-de-Port. At Hiriburia the routes from Paris, Vezalay and Le Puy meet. A place of significance where one can imagine the pilgrims of old coming from different parts of France would have merged and continued together their walk to the Pyrenees. My route from Le Puy was known as the Via Podiensis, the route from Vezalay the Via Lemovicensis, and from Paris the Via Turonensis.

The *Société des Amis de Saint Jacques* have erected a small monument, known as Stele de Gibralta. Nothing to do with the British enclave in the south of Spain, the name is derived from a basque word. I continued up a long hill along a track named the *Chemin de Procession* to the Chapelle de Soyarza, a modern building (1894) replacing a much older oratory dedicated to Notre Dame. A small covered shrine provided a rest area and an opportunity to admire the superb views of the countryside.

I descended to the village of Uhart-Mixe where I stayed at the *Gîte d'étape l'Escargot*, which was also a café bar and provided space for camping.

I shared a little cabin with split doors out the back with Klaus. He had very little French or English. However, he explained to me that he had started from Lake Constance but his knee was playing up and he might have to stop. His worst days were when he covered thirty kilometres or more. On the days that he walked twenty kilometres his knee was okay. He puzzled me. Why not just walk twenty kilometres every day and eventually get there?

A young Dutch lad Jan who was two metres tall had started at Amsterdam. He had excellent English. He was studying engineering but didn't like it so he took to the Camino. He was aiming for Santiago. He had little money so he had his own tent. Three French ladies completed the dinner table. The linguistic skills of one impressed me; she spoke excellent English and German. We had some lovely word plays.

I had used the French word *judicieusement* (judiciously) to describe the way I walked with frequent rests. I pronounced every syllable carefully – *judiciesement et doucement* (gently). She thought it was a lovely word and rolled it around and around. I'm sure she was an actor, she had such an expressive face.

We had a lot of fun and with the variety of languages everyone was included. Klaus had already retired when I came to bed. He must have been tired as he was an excellent snorer. I never found out if he continued. His was one of many whose story I never heard the end of. It was frustrating sometimes, like reading a book with the last chapters missing.

Friday I set off early a little sad yet relieved that this was my last full day of walking. I had barely left the *gîte* when I ran into a herd of cows being shepherded by a large dog. The dog decided to include me and I found myself being herded along. Along came the farmer following on a tractor. He yelled to the dog and to me telling me not to be afraid of the dog. I wasn't, I replied and the dog let me go on my way and concentrated on his cows.

After the plains of Aquitane and the monotony of Landes, the Basque country was a green countryside with abundant vegetation. I stopped frequently to admire the view as the Pyrenees loomed larger. A series of peaks extended to the left, the right and to the front. No doubt they were a formidable barrier in earlier centuries and are still challenging today if you're planning to walk over them. This is an area of France where they expect 250 days of rain each year. I was in the foothills so

I had to climb plenty of hills, always a challenge. I passed many typically basque houses, with their white walls, flat roofs and balconies of wood painted red.

After forty-seven days of walking my body was tired and tender. Earlier in the Camino when others asked me how far I was planning to walk I would sometimes reply that I was planning to stop at Saint-Jean-Pied-de-Port but if I had the energy I would cross the Pyrenees and cease walking at Pamplona. I reckoned that by the time I reached the Pyrenees I would be track-hardened and able to run up the mountains. People would divide the number of days left into the distance to be covered and conclude that I could easily reach Pamplona.

Before I left Australia I had booked a seat on the train to Paris for Saturday, the following afternoon. Because the ticket had been so cheap, I thought of forfeiting and purchasing another ticket later. I still had three weeks before my return flight to Sydney. I had plenty of time to walk to Pamplona if I wished. The nearer I got to the Pyrenees the louder I could hear my body complaining: 'Noel, you're not ready to tackle the Pyrenees. Your body's done enough. You've reached your objective of arriving at Saint-Jean-Pied-de-Port. Be satisfied. That's enough.' I could hear Maris agreeing. I listened, a major lesson of the Camino, because in fits of bravado, I sometimes attempt more than my body is prepared to handle.

On my last night on the road, I went upmarket and stopped at the *chambre et table d'hôtes Ferme Etxekonia* at Bussunartis. As I was the only guest that night the owner Marie brought me into the kitchen to dine with the family, which consisted of Marie and her daughter. I could hear Celeste singing and at first assumed she was a small child. She was thirty-years-old and had Down's Syndrome.

Marie and I had the opportunity for extended conversation.

She gave me a good account of the Basque culture. She spoke the language and to demonstrate its importance tuned into a number of TV and radio stations broadcasting in Basque. She also spoke of the difficulties in caring for a handicapped child. Celeste chatted away, called me 'Pèlerin'(pilgrim) and from her affection I could see the love that existed between mother and child. In the morning I was touched by her farewell. She gave me a hug and kissed me on both cheeks. In that simple affection I felt complete acceptance.

Shortly after leaving Celeste and Marie I arrived at Saint Jean-le-Vieux. I stopped at the church of Saint-Pierre. Typical of Basque churches, galleries on two levels surrounded three sides of the nave. I paused at the smaller church of Saint Mary-Madeleine where I lit my last candles and gave thanks that I had almost made it. Only a few kilometres! It did not take long to traverse the final four kilometres to Saint-Jean-Pied-de-Port, a small border town on the river Nive.

I entered by the Porte Saint-Jacques at the top of the ancient cobbled Rue de la Citadelle, stopped by at the pilgrim information office (*Acceuil Pèlerin de l'Association des Amis de Saint-Jacques des Pyrenees Atlantiques*) and had my *crédenciale* stamped for the last time. The office was full of pilgrims who were about to begin. For a moment I thought I should continue on with them and cross the Pyrenees to Pamplona.

I consulted my body and it screamed 'No!' It had had enough. For now.

Saint-Jean-Pied-de-Port was a junction in my journey. I visited the railway station with the intention of reserving a ticket for Monday before checking into a *gîte* for two nights but I discovered that the train to Bayonne was due to leave and would arrive in time to catch the TGV to Paris. My reservation was for that train. So instead of staying the weekend in

Saint-Jean-Pied-de-Port, I took the train to Bayonne and then to Paris. My Camino was over, all its brouhaha gone, wrenched abruptly from me. I was no longer a pilgrim. Somewhere around Dax I packed away my pilgrim shell, and replaced my broad pilgrim hat with my tourist cap.

I wanted to do a number of trips out of Paris. However, the railway unions were talking tough. You were never sure of the rolling strikes and if you took a trip whether the trains would get you back. I risked the ride to Chartres. I walked the labyrinth in the magnificent cathedral in 2006 and was keen to walk again. My mind was full of my pilgrimage. I had walked through France and as I walked the labyrinth, I asked myself, *What had happened to my heart and soul?* I felt a strong bond with my fellow pilgrims.

Through their footprints on the track, I felt a connection with those who had walked a day or two before me, as if they had left something of their essence behind just as my footprints would be left for those after me to follow. I thought of those who had walked the same route a thousand years before and the millions in between. I was part of an enormous community stretching down the centuries all with the same objective of searching for something bigger than themselves (I called it God) and the spirit of Saint James. All creation, all living creatures, all people of all ages are interconnected and interdependent. That was one of the most valuable spiritual insights I received on the Camino.

The Camino taught me many lessons. The first was to travel lightly, applicable not only to the Camino but to life as well. The second was to take one day at a time and then to commit to it. This is the lesson I have to remind myself of all the time. I find myself fretting about some future event when I should be prepared to trust in God. What I worry about never happens anyway. Make your plans but be prepared for the unforseen. A third lesson was to keep things simple. A fourth is to face up to situations and don't shy away from the difficult path. Remember my Cs and Ss. Meet challenges with courage, conviction, compassion, constancy rather than with concern for safety, security or social conformity. Be open to every experience but listen to my body. It knows what I am capable of, much better than me.

Had I grown spiritually? A healthy spirituality has many qualities. Self-acceptance, self-esteem, patience, courage, perseverance, acceptance of others, love, friendship, hospitality, forgiveness, generosity and gratitude are just a few. Then there's an openness to new ideas, a willingness to learn and to change, tolerance of the differences in others, joy and playfulness, hope, a sense of freedom, a desire for balance and variety. I'd like to think that every step I took on the Camino, every encounter with my fellow pilgrims, every moment of reflection, all the chaos and creativity of my journey contributed to my spiritual growth.

Entr'acte

11. Ce que est très dur rend très fort

(What is very hard makes one very strong)

Back in Paris I was sitting in the Luxemburg Gardens one day watching the passers-by, most of whom were tourists. A piece of advice my daughter Angela regularly gave me was, 'Dad, merge in. Look like a local.' I must have been successful, an old bloke sunning himself in the park, as people were asking me directions, sometimes in French and sometimes in English.

A dark young man loomed out of the crowd, sat on the seat beside me and asked in English if I spoke English. He seemed exhausted and desperate. I had to help him, he said. He had been in France five days, three of them in jail. They were going to deport him. He was from Sri Lanka. He was a Tamil and in the war both his father and brother were killed. He had no French, no friends; nobody liked him here in France. They hated him and wanted to get rid of him. I had to help him, he repeated.

I felt helpless. I wracked my brain but nothing emerged. What could I do except to talk to him in English and encourage him? I usually have no trouble finding words, but this time I was dumb and speechless. He sat for a while muttering he needed help, I had to help him. He got up and dashed back into the crowd and I watched him hurrying into nowhere. I felt pathetic. A suffering fellow human was asking me for help. I wanted to help and I hadn't a clue what to do.

I guess I was like the rest of Europe, faced with an insolvable problem. I had made contact in a tiny way with the massive challenge facing Europe in the way of illegal immigration. As a tourist it's easy to see the facade and gloss over the real problems.

❖

A few days after I arrived home, I drove to Queensland to spend a week with my sister Maria. By that time it was four months since her husband, Joe, had died.

Conscious that I had missed the funeral I rang Maria regularly while in France so I was now able to spend the time with her and give her support by just hanging out with her, pottering around and doing a few jobs. Her grief was raw and she missed Joe badly. So many of the tasks that he used to perform she had to do herself.

Back in Sydney I approached the retirement village three kilometres up the road. I had driven past Glenaeon on the way to church every week and both Maris and I thought it could be an option as we aged. I am sure that we would have been there earlier had she lived. A number of two bedroom units were available. The one that appealed faced the bush.

Glenaeon is situated on the edge of a national park. Moving to Glenaeon had many advantages. I would be moving only three kilometres so I would still be living in a familiar area. I would go to the same church and visit the same shops. I took out an option.

Six years after Maris' death, I was ready to leave my house, the home where Maris and I reared our family. I had been contemplating the move before I left for Europe but I made the decision on the Camino, not in one instant but gradually the idea evolved as I moved across France. By the time I reached Saint Jean-Pied-de-Port, I had resolved to make inquiries on my return.

Thus began the job of de-cluttering. The accumulated stuff of thirty years had to be reduced. I had to remove the rest of Maris' clothes. I had needed to hang on to them but six years after her death, I was ready to be separated. I was about to apply two lessons of the Camino. The first was to travel lightly, the second was to keep life simple. I didn't need a five bedroom house. I could quite easily fit into a two bedroom unit with all the stuff I needed.

In the meantime I was back at the gym. Jenni, my personal trainer, was pleased to see me back intact, looking fitter and healthier. That didn't stop her from working me hard. The gym ran a competition: Member for the Month and Member for the Year. Jenni wanted to nominate me for Member of the Year.

I was rather bemused that an old bloke – probably one of the oldest – should be considered when the people who attend the gym are of all ages from teenagers. She said I was an inspiration and gave my story to management.

I am 77 years. I have been thinking about the pilgrimage walk through France for over ten years but actually have been preparing myself physically for at least two years. I attended the gym regularly and also did a walk through the Flinders Ranges in September 2009 and rode a bike from Launceston to Hobart in February 2010. I was keen to be as fit and healthy as possible. I am grateful to Jenni for the programme she developed to strengthen my leg muscles. I attended cycle and yoga classes. I went for long walks in the district. I followed an ancient pilgrimage route through France, I chose the route that begins at Le-Puy-en-Velay in Eastern France and walked to the Spanish border, a distance of 760 kilometres. I walked for 48 days averaging 16 kilometres per day, wearing a backpack of 12 kilos. The route was hilly, the highest point being about 1200 metres and the lowest about 60 metres. I did the walk for the physical challenge and also for spiritual reasons. I lost 4 cm around the waist, 5 kilos of weight and 6% body fat. I am thankful for the health and fitness that allowed me to tackle this challenge while others of my age can't even walk across the room.

The challenge is not yet finished. There's more to come. I'm hopeful of continuing the pilgrimage in 2011, commencing where I stopped and continuing over the Pyrenees through Spain to Santiago, another 760 kilometres. I will continue with a gym programme that maintains my fitness and allows me to continue the pilgrimage with confidence.

At the Christmas party at the local pub where a few of the gym members engaged in the process of undoing the year's hard work on their bodies, the gym manager Gareth read out the stories of the members in the contest. I found their accounts fascinating. All indicated significant achievement. Some had fought the hard battle of recovery from injury and illness. Others had come from obesity to considerable weight loss. All stories indicated the power of the human spirit to meet challenges and overcome difficulties, as spiritual an endeavour as you're likely to hear. I felt humbled and privileged.

I was waiting to hear my story and as Gareth got down to the last few I knew I was a contender. He read the story of Catherine, the female Member of the Year. After devoting her total attention to the care of a very sick child, she felt so fat and

unfit when she came to the gym but regained the confidence
to work hard on her rehabilitation.

Finally Gareth got around to reading my story. I was the
male Member of the Year for 2010. It was sinking in that
perhaps my achievement could be inspiring to others. I
remembered the young Brazilian at the language school at
Amboise hoping that he would like me when he was my age,
as did Boris who shared a room with me at Saugues.

Now younger gym members were congratulating me and
saying the same thing. It was nice to think that I was a model
for young people. I did not fit into the stereotype of how older
people behave. I gave a short speech of thanks. What I wanted
to do was to give God a rap, that God had given me the genes
and the strength. Instead I thanked Jenni for her care and
attention and accepted my prize, a mountain bicycle which,
as I had walked to the hotel where the party was being held, I
was able to ride home.

Fiona, the real estate agent, who was organising the sale of
the house, ran a few advertisements and open houses and set
up a website. I didn't expect much response right on Christmas but nevertheless the people turned up to view the house.

As this was the year that the kids went to the in-laws for
Christmas I spent the festive season with Maria and her family
in Queensland. Back in Sydney in the New Year, Fiona took up
the sales campaign and soon I had an acceptable offer. Then
began the process of getting rid of so much stuff. Most items
were easy to chuck out, but others were loaded with sentiment,
such as two Rembrandt prints which Maris and I purchased in
our first year of marriage. I placed them in beautifully carved
old frames I found in my mother's house .

I moved into my new home. Friends were telling me I had
made the right decision and chosen the right time. I had the

strength and health to undergo the stress of moving house and would have settled into a new place before old age caught up. People, they said, often leave the move until they are sick and feeble. Fortunately or thanks to God I was not on the sick and feeble list.

I had an irresistible desire to return and continue the journey to Santiago. I had experienced something greater than myself, something that challenged me, pushed me hard and enlightened me. I would have been frustrated and angry if, say, a change in my health prevented me from taking on the physical demands. At the moment, I was fine, but I had to admit time was starting to run out.

At seventy-eight years of age, I wasn't exactly on the home run to the grave and to joining Maris, but if I were going to do something physically challenging I'd need to do it soon.

Nine months after I had returned to Sydney from Europe, I was back on the plane to Paris.

Act Two

Spain
El Camino de Santiago
de Compostela

12. Reaching all the way to the heavens

The night before I left I stayed with my daughter Angela. I woke at 2.30 am and dozed until the alarm rang at 4.30. In that dark space of two hours I tossed and turned in the child's bed that my granddaughter Eliza had given up for her pa. My mind raced with negative thoughts. The time for departure had arrived too quickly. I was reluctant. I was leaving my comfortable life in my new home where I had lived a mere three months. Now I was embracing the unknown. I tried to remind myself that I knew about the Camino from experience. I asked myself why I was doing this.

'It helps to be mad,' I had said to my daughter Angela the night before.

'Dad, it's adventurous.'

Climbing the Pyrenees was foremost in my mind. A lot of effort went into preparing my body. I had visited the gym three to four times per week and walked many kilometres. I was not concerned about my feet or legs as I hadn't suffered a single blister in France. However, the muscles across my back used to ache from the weight of my backpack. I concentrated on strengthening my shoulder and back muscles.

Remembering the lessons of France I gave careful consideration to my baggage. *Travel lightly* was the maxim. I was fit and healthy. I felt like an athlete ready for the race. I thanked God for my health and fitness.

I was thankful for qualities of the spirit, such as a sense of curiosity and adventure, readiness to step out of my comfort zone. I considered my own spirituality, developed and changing over time, a reflection of my whole being and shaped by multiple factors such as my temperament, age, life experience (particularly the life and death of Maris) and my rearing in the Catholic tradition. Returning to the Camino was like an unfaltering spiritual flame. I was continuing my journey of self-discovery, of pushing beyond my limits, of seeking connection with the world around me and with the Great Mystery known as God.

I said goodbye to Maris. I visited her grave in its beautiful bushland setting in the Frenchs Forest Bushland Cemetery.

MARIS CATHERINE BRAUN
Died 30th October 2004, aged 66 years.
Cherished wife of Noel (Sweetheart)
Mother of Angela, Jacinta, Stephen & Tim
Gran to Tessa, Hugh, Eliza & Brody
Loved by her family and many friends

When I'm home I visit her grave weekly with fresh flowers, usually orchids or carnations because they last longer. No plastic flowers for my Maris! I like to sit on an adjacent seat, installed by a family whose son fell fatally out of a tree, feel the sun on my back, listen to the birds and the breeze stirring the gum trees and talk to her, telling her the news of the week. I think of my three grandchildren – Abigail, Oscarine and Augustine – who have arrived since her death. She has missed the joy of seeing them grow up and they have missed her loving care.

I planned to travel on her birthday but the travel agent came up with a cheap flight on the Sunday. I set out two days earlier and would begin walking on her birthday – a fitting tribute as I dedicated the walk to her. This would be my fourth overseas trip since she died. I had a recurring dream in which she returned. I felt great joy at seeing her. Her presence seemed so strong that when I woke I couldn't locate myself, couldn't find a way to where I was, when I was, who I was. Then the confusion was usurped by the bitter taste of disappointment. I would do anything to have her back. She was travelling with me in spirit.

Maris' birthday was 26th July. She would have been seventy-three. How different my life would be if she were alive. I would not have been in Paris, getting ready to embark south to resume my walking. I would have been in Sydney, caring for Maris whose body and mind may have deteriorated under the ravages of depression. Or she may have recovered and we could have enjoyed together travelling in another part. Who knows?

At the Gare Montparnasse I took the TGV to Bayonne, a four hour trip. As we travelled south it started to rain. That was disappointing as I was hoping for a dry start to my walking. The rain drops travelling across the windows reminded me of sperm and of new life. They reminded me of the many times Maris and I made love and of our children. It was dark by the time I reached Bayonne. I had booked the Hotel Cote Basque by internet because it was close to the railway station. It was only 100 metres away but it was a dingy affair with dark wood panelling and low wattage lights. Rain fell during the night but stopped for my morning walk in the grey light back to the railway station. The sky was dark and threatening more rain.

The train ride from Bayonne to Saint-Jean-Pied-de-Port was about one hour. Most of my fellow passengers had backpacks. They were all young. I was probably more than fifty years their senior. I should have been on a cruise or a coach tour in the company of others my age, but here I was surrounded by adventurers. Rain fell. Most of the passengers had descended at a previous station, so only a handful walked with me up the hill to the town. The steep walk up rue de la Citadelle to the *Centre d'acceuil Saint-Jacques* was familiar. I was greeted by a warm friendly Frenchman who gave me my *crédenciale* and track notes for the Pyrenees.

I walked down rue de la Citadelle on the first steps of my 760 kilometres journey, careful not to slip on the wet paving stones. What an irony to lose my footing in the first few metres and break a leg! The Frenchman came running after me with my *crédenciale*, which I had left on his desk. My learning had begun. Lesson One: Always check that you have everything.

The cobbled paving stones, medieval houses and evidence of earlier fortifications indicated the history of Saint-Jean-Pied-de-Port. This little town was an important means of passage into the Iberian Peninsula and has seen in the course of its history many conquering armies. At first, the Romans, then the Germains and the Visigoths, but, most importantly, Charlemagne and his army. Everyone had to pass through Saint-Jean before going on to wage war on the other side of the Pyrenees, so it changed hands a few times down the centuries.

Not that I gave history much thought as I walked down rue de la Citadelle, visited the church Notre-Dame-au-Bout-du-Pont, crossed the bridge and up the hill to the edge of town.

My guidebook divided the way to Santiago into thirty-one stages (one stage per day). The first stage was from Saint-Jean-Pied-de-Port to Roncevaux (Roncesvalles in Spanish), a distance of twenty-seven kilometres.

Two possibilities presented themselves. One could go over the mountain by the Route Napoleon or take the Route Nationale walking along the road. If the weather was uncertain, the guidebook recommended accepting the warnings from the *acceuil Saint-Jacques* and taking the Route Nationale. Despite the rain and the threat of more, my Frenchman had given no such warning.

As I left the town, I came across a notice explaining the two possible routes: over the tough mountains or along the flat route. The notice also issued a warning to the effect that only the fit and healthy should take the walk over the Pyrenees. That was a challenge I could not reject. Hadn't I been training for the last nine months with traversing the Pyrenees in mind, the most difficult section of the walk?

I took to the left and began the ascent. The rain had held off since I left the train but now it fell. I was hoping for a dry start but it was not to be so I had to stop and extract my wet weather gear. As I climbed the view became more spectacular, my reward for getting wet. The higher I climbed the smaller the roads, houses and farms became as they receded behind me and the country stretched out like a map. I would have appreciated a bright sun and a clear blue sky but had to do with the dark clouds that menaced with more rain.

My guidebook also warned me not to set out from Saint-Jean-Pied-de-Port after 10.00 am because it took eight to nine hours of walking to reach Roncevaux – more likely ten hours plus for me as steep climbs are always a challenge. I knew that I would be leaving the starting point late so I had booked by internet the night for the *Refuge-Auberge* at Orisson, a distance of eight kilometres, just on the French side of the border. Consequently, the day was easy because of the short distance but difficult because of the rain and steep climb.

The *auberge* was an oasis in the middle of nowhere. There was nothing except for a few damp sheep but as I rounded a bend in the track, there it was. Opposite the *auberge* was a platform built over the slope which provided a magnificent view of the valley and of a hillside dotted with sheep and horses.

I shared a room with three others – a young man Peter from Austria, Evelyn who was French and a German girl who knew Sydney. All of us had started that day and were hoping to get to Santiago but everyone was apprehensive about whether they had the courage and fitness to complete the Camino.

All the guests sat down together to dinner – twenty-five of us, of all ages. I was reminded of the instant camaraderie and many wonderful evenings I spent the previous year. We were invited to introduce ourselves.

One by one we stood and spoke in a variety of languages of where we were from, about where we had started walking and how far we hoped to get. It was a wonderful way to get to know each other and to develop a sense of community which was to last for several days as I met again and again my fellow diners.

The evening reminded me of how the Camino works. The Camino eliminates differences between people of different ages, classes and nationalities. The normal barriers are thrown aside as a feeling of unity and connectedness brings people together in a way that seems impossible within the routines of everyday life. For a little while, a pilgrim is separate and apart from the usual life's demands and expectations. It's like being in an in-between space offering great transition and potential to learn and experience things which really matter.

I began my first full day of walking with a meal of bread and jam, a breakfast I never got used to all the time I was in France. The beautiful views of the previous day were shrouded in fog and it was eerie to watch the walkers in front of me disappearing into the mist. The track seemed to climb into nowhere and with a few metres of visibility I was thankful for the frequent markers.

I climbed in my usual slow fashion with many pauses to regain my breath. Judicious rests I called them. In France I used to say I had stopped to catch the views but I had only a blank white wall of mist to stare into. A passing walker joked about the magnificent view I was admiring.

Everyone who had stayed at Orisson had left me behind and after an hour or so, pilgrims who had started that morning at Saint-Jean-Pied-de-Port passed me. Occasionally the mist lifted just enough to give me a glimpse of what I was missing. The track was muddy. At times I felt as if I would be taking half of France clinging to my boots into Spain.

Throughout the long misty morning I struggled up the mountain track, feeling I was engulfed both by fog and a task that was growing too large for me but, eventually, the way levelled. I had reached the top. I had climbed the Pyrenees. I had climbed 1200 metres from Saint Jean-Pied-de-Port. A 12th century pilgrims' guide describes the Pyrenees as the greatest work of nature on the way to Santiago. The author writes:

> Its height is so great that it seems to reach all the way to the heavens – to the person ascending it seems that he himself is able to reach with his own hands.

Only 765 kilometres to Santiago a milepost told me.

Shortly after, on the edge of France, a van complete with awning was offering food and drinks. The enterprising owner had written a list of countries on the door and was marking the countries of origin of the walkers. I was the only Australian for the day. Greetings in many languages covered the side panel. I added, *G'day, Mate!*

There was nothing to distinguish my entry into Spain, just a muddy track and a cattle grid as if the two countries were keen to keep out each other's animals. Yet, it was a route followed by millions of pilgrims down the ages. In the misty silence I listened for the first sounds of Spain and heard only a rustling stillness as if the spirits of ancient pilgrims were still passing.

The descent to Roncesvalles was steep and tortuous. The abbey of Our Lady was established in the early 12th century. It served as a hospice because thousands of pilgrims had lost their lives in the snow, their bodies eaten by wolves. It became one of the great pilgrim hospices of the Middle Ages.

I encountered neither snow nor wolves. My danger lay in the loose rocks which could have sent me sliding on a path of destruction and a sojourn in a Spanish hospital with a broken leg.

I arrived intact at the *Albergue de la Collegiate Real* which offered places for up to 400. The size was overwhelming – in sharp contrast to the smaller French *gîtes*. Priority was given to pilgrims arriving by foot, so I and many others from a host of countries were warmly received by the *hospitaleros*.

I was impressed by the number of languages my *hospitalero* spoke. As I sat in the courtyard in the warm Spanish sun, I was pleased with myself. I had conquered the Pyrenees even though I had taken two days when most walkers take one. I was surprised at the large crowd of pilgrims in the *albergue*. There seemed nowhere near that number walking over the mountains from France, but, after talking to others, I realised that most had taken the easier option, missed the Pyrenees and were starting at Roncesvalles. I kid you not.

Everyone crowded into the church for Mass and a pilgrims' blessing. I didn't understand a word but the service was easy to follow. When I heard the word 'Australian' I guessed the priest was reading the list of countries of those present.

I found the ceremony very moving. I imagined that the congregation ranged in belief from devout Catholics to non-believers who attended because it was part of the pilgrimage, but all were united in a common spiritual quest of working towards their unique potential, as if they were being called to become all that God had made them to be.

Not everyone would use that language but the congregation seemed to be in silent communication with each other, supporting each other. Each had their own intensely personal journey but all were united in gaining some understanding of themselves in the intensely physical challenge of climbing mountains and walking across endless plains under the hot Spanish sun. Hopefully, the mutual support would heighten each person's awareness of their own ideals and values and deter them from giving up when the journey became difficult or confusing. Their physical and interior spiritual journeys were in dialogue.

The interior of the *albergue* had been renovated and what was once a huge dormitory had been modernised and divided into cubicles of four. I had been allocated a top bunk. My three companions were Spanish with no English so our conversation was limited. My first night in Spain was remarkable for the vicious toilets which, because of the large number of pilgrims, flushed stridently all night. I noted the lessons to be learned for the future. Always ask for a lower bunk and try not to get too close to the toilets.

The walking was easy, along neat well-formed and well-maintained paths, downhill all the way with a couple of sharp rises. I kept meeting the people from the first night. I met a Spanish family from Madrid. They were friendly, impressed that I was going as far as Santiago and knew enough English for some conversation. They taught me a few phrases such as *¿De donde eras?*(Where are you from?) and *¿A donde vas?*(Where are you going?). I was to use those phrases frequently.

I visited my first Spanish bar at Espinal. According to my guidebook, the bar is an institution in the land of Iberia. A Spaniard without a bar falls into deep depression. That's why I would find a plethora of them along the Camino. They sell food as well as drinks. The lady was severe with me for not pronouncing understandable Spanish but eventually worked out I wanted a *bocadillo con jamon* (ham roll) for my breakfast.

The *albergue* was almost full by the time I arrived at Zubiri (twenty-two kilometres). After the effort of the last two days and the interrupted sleep, my body was tired and I was more than happy to stop. I shared a dormitory with Peter and Evelyn along with many others.

I visited my second bar and had a couple of beers with Peter. He had reasonable English and told me he was twenty-four and was hoping the Camino would help him to find himself as he felt he had no goals. He had a goal of downing lots of beer and wanted me to join him, but I left him for dinner at a nearby restaurant and shared the table with Evelyn, an Irish lady by the name of Siobhan, and three Portuguese, a personable young man named Rua, a priest and a young girl who was accompanying him. Rua was proficient in a number of languages.

The conversation was vigorous and focussed on the disaffection with the Church among many Catholics in Europe. I mentioned there were plenty of disaffected Catholics in Australia. Rua was quite passionate and outspoken; he said he used to be a brother in the Taizé Community, which I was to visit later. I translated the gist of the conversation into French for Evelyn.

Back at the *albergue*, people were enjoying the balmy evening in the courtyard. So many nationalities, so many languages! I tried conversing with a number of Spaniards. I was surprised how far we got. The dormitory had twenty-eight beds. It was a squash but people respected each other. I didn't expect to sleep but, in actual fact, I slept soundly.

People began stirring shortly after 5.00 am and were packing in the dark or by the light of a torch. In the cramped conditions with very little space even to put down your backpack it was easy enough for you to gather up someone else's belongings. However, I had everything when I left.

For a while the Camino followed a very attractive shaded path by a river where pilgrims had taken the opportunity to rest and bathe their feet. I kept coming across Evelyn as well as the Portuguese priest and his companion. I spoke to many others. Most were friendly and responded to my greeting. I was feeling chirpy so I was greeting them with all the languages I knew: *Hola! Bonjour! Guten Tag! Hello! G'day!* That was a quick way of working out the language. If they spoke English or French, I could converse easily enough. I would farewell people similarly: *Hasta Luego! A bientot! Bis Spater! See you later!*

A few were unresponsive. They seem to isolate themselves and the wall they had built around themselves was almost visible. Such people puzzled me. Was the Camino a silent retreat for them, or were they shy or absorbed in their own troubles? A German boy told me he was from Strasburg. He said he was okay but his body language suggested that he was not enjoying the Camino. He seemed sad and dejected and even the shell hanging from his backpack was broken.

At one of my rests, I met a group of three blokes. We passed each other during the day. They were very friendly and intrigued that I had come all the way from Australia. Two were Spanish and the other was Argentinian. They had enough English to make conversation worthwhile. One of the Spanish was named Denis. He had long ginger hair and beard, a leather hat, the baggiest of ragged shorts and wore a notice on his backpack: *Tarot cards read.* I sensed he belonged to the Brotherhood of Camino Characters. I said goodbye to Denis and his two mates on the outskirts of Pamplona. He wanted a photo of me and him together because he thought I was the character. I, too, was of the Brotherhood.

Last year I spent three weeks at Amboise enrolled in a French language school before travelling to Le Puy-en-Velay. This year I had decided to stop at Pamplona to learn Spanish. Not that I would learn much in two weeks but at least I would develop enough confidence to ask questions or begin a conversation. I could never hope to gain the same level of competence as I had in French. I was sad leaving my new friends. I guessed I would meet others and, who knows, I could meet them again on the road.

I can't say I wasn't displeased to be stopping; fatigue was eating my bones. I needed a rest.

13. Because I'm in Spain

I was enrolled at the Pamplona Spanish Learning Institute and was to stay with a host family. I rang them on Thursday and in my very broken Spanish told them I would arrive Sunday afternoon (*Domingo a la tarde*). I could hear a lot of conversation and laughter in the background. I didn't understand a word of the woman's reply so I hoped she got the message. I obtained a map of Pamplona at the tourist bureau and found my way to their house, a large two story house surrounded by a garden.

Jacinto and Loli were open and welcoming. They had no English or French. They were very patient while I tried to find the right word from my limited Spanish vocabulary. We enjoyed a hilarious afternoon misunderstanding each other. Dinner was at 9.00 pm so I had time for a siesta. We continued our conversation over dinner. Communication was slow and laboured. There were moments of enlightenment and joy when they understood me. I went to bed with the thought that, even if I learn nothing in the two weeks, it should be fun.

The language school was housed in an imposing prosperous 19th century building just around the corner from the house. I was placed in an advanced beginners' class. My classmates were Japanese, Taiwanese and German, all in their teens or early twenties, so I gave them fifty years plus. The age difference didn't seem to matter; I was a student just like them struggling with the Spanish language, no different to when I was learning French at Chambéry and Amboise. Classes were from 9.00 am to 1.00 pm so the afternoon was free.

On Monday afternoon I wandered around the town. Along

the Camino the pilgrim moves from place to place, spending a night here and a night there, taking small bites, as it were, like eating a tapas, and moving on. But here in Pamplona I was pausing for a full meal. I would get to know the city's quirks and feel the rhythm of its life.

Pamplona is a beautiful city with lots of history. The fiesta of San Fernin was over and they had just finished running the bulls. So that's a challenge I didn't have to accept. San Fermin is a major festival and I saw a countdown clock ticking away the seconds until next year's. I was conscious that I had shed my pilgrim identity. For the moment I was a tourist but, as I saw pilgrims with backpacks (*mochilas*) walking through the town, I consoled myself with the thought that I would soon re-join them.

It was a long afternoon until dinner. As well as misunderstandings being humorous, I was frustrated at not being able to communicate adequately. Normally I converse easily. Now I was powerless, just like any traveller who finds himself confronted with an unfamiliar language. I felt isolated in my non-understanding. Perhaps the sense of isolation is part of the pilgrim's lot. He's a stranger in a strange land where the people have a strange language and customs.

On Tuesday a new student joined our class. Lukas was fourteen from Germany and was studying Spanish during his school holidays to improve his grades at school. Strange, I thought, that a fourteen-year-old wanted to sit in a class when most of his contemporaries preferred the beach. In the afternoon, one of the teachers took the new students on a guided tour of Pamplona. There's an arena for the bullfights but Carmen, our teacher/guide, told us that they only have bullfights during the festival. They ran the bulls at 8.00 am every day for two weeks – five tame white ones who lead the way and five wild ones who meet their fate in the bull ring that afternoon while the white ones live for the next day.

This is the town that Hemingway made famous and the town acknowledges it. Carmen took us to a bar where a life-sized statue leans on the counter. I drank a beer in Hemingway's memory. Carmen pointed out to me a fountain notorious for the number of Australians who climb it and jump off during the San Fermin festival. One of the other students asked me why I was learning Spanish.

I replied, 'Because I'm in Spain.'

After the tour, I wandered through the town. There was a lot to see. The shops close from 2.00–5.00 pm and then stay open into the night. In fact, the town seems to come alive as the evening advances.

By the end of the week I had settled into a routine. Classes went from 9.00 am to 1.30 pm. I felt inadequate in my struggles with the Spanish language. The teachers were very helpful. Gemma had a wicked sense of humour which made her lessons fun. She was very gentle in her criticisms, and impressed that I had paused for two weeks in Pamplona before continuing the Camino. She believed she did not have the physical or emotional strength to undertake such a venture. Noela was young, very enthusiastic about her teaching and she put a lot of effort and preparation into her lessons. I often had difficulty in understanding and the other students had to help me. I felt uncomfortable. I like to be self-sufficient and to work things out for myself. I could have easily been embarrassed when I didn't understand, but I decided there was no point in being embarrassed. Just accept the help.

As well as learning Spanish, classes were a lesson in humility, having to rely on others when I didn't understand. I was just a student and a slow one at that. I had been stripped of my usual identity. No one knew me and my background. My family and support networks were on the other side of the world. I felt naked and vulnerable. Although I was not walking, I was still a pilgrim venturing into the unknown, having to depend on others for support. The students were keen to help.

Lukas, the fourteen-year-old German, was very good to me. He was familiar with four languages – German, English, Spanish and a German dialect. He was very ordered and organised, but, like many other fourteen-year-olds, he loved to tell me jokes in English. I dug into my memory for some old schoolboy jokes. He loved to hear them. I could imagine him back home in Germany telling those Aussie yarns to his mates

After 1.30 pm, the rest of the day was my own. It was a long day, waiting until 9.00 pm or later for dinner. I got to know Pamplona and its parks, the shops and points of interest.

On a number of afternoons I had to fight against boredom. I found myself inactive, filling in time until dinner. Perhaps, this was also part of my pilgrimage, my spiritual journey. There would be periods of activity and periods of doing nothing. My restless nature made me uncomfortable with inactivity. I had forfeited my freedom when I joined Jacinto and Loli. I felt trapped in the routines of the household and part of that was having dinner late. That, of course, is the Spanish custom.

I saw many walkers in the afternoon as I dawdled around town, not wishing to return home too early. I was envious of them and was keen to start walking again. It seemed ridiculous as I would be on the way in only a few days. I was learning new lessons. I had to be patient and to wait. I had to let go of my desire to fill the day. Forced inactivity was a challenge. I don't have to rush and fill every moment of the day. That was another lesson I had to learn.

I must have learned some Spanish. When I asked for a

beer (*una cervesa, per favor*) the first time, the bartender didn't understand. By now, I was able to give my order and be confident of getting my drink. Every Spaniard has his bar and by now I had selected my favourite. The bar Media Luna was like a kiosk in the Parque de la Media Luna. It was the nearest to the language school and to Loli and Jacinto's.

After class I would call in for some lunch, wander into town and call in for a beer before returning home. The garden was formally laid out and it was peaceful to sit by the water with my beer and watch the carp nosing their way through the pond. Another favourite place was the Plaza de Castillo. It was nice to sit in the sun, or if the day was too hot, in the shade of one of the buildings and watch the ever-changing scene.

Pilgrims with their backpacks crossed the square, tourists sauntered eating their ice creams or photographing everything, young men rode their skateboards, children played near the fountain. Numerous bars fronted the plaza with hundreds of seats and patrons. One of the bars was Hemingway's favourite.

I tested my Spanish when I needed some eardrops to clear a blockage. Before entering the chemist, I wrote in my notebook that I had a blocked right ear. Did they have ear drops which might clear it or soften the wax? The chemist knew exactly what I wanted and suggested a spray. He had just a little English and complemented me on preparing myself so well. I noted that many of the tourists spoke to the shopkeepers in English, as if expecting them to know the language. Some did but most didn't. I always spoke in Spanish and if I got lost I somehow muddled through.

On the last day at the school, I was surprised at how emotional Gemma was. She seemed to have developed an attachment to me. As I sat in the class for the last lessons, I wondered whether stopping in Pamplona had been a good thing or not. I found myself under attack. Anxiety had unleashed itself and threatened to undermine me. I was distracted from the lesson fighting off the assault. What I was worried about was hard to pin down – just a vague apprehension. Was I worried that I'd have trouble finding a bed on the crowded Camino? I had become comfortable in Pamplona and now I was moving out of my comfort zone again. I had met Jacinto and Loli, my teachers, Gemma and Noela, and my fellow students, all of them good people, and now I was leaving them, just like I left Denis and his mates. Now I would repeat the entire process of meeting new walkers. I had to remind myself that I usually have no trouble meeting people. I had to remind myself that what will happen will happen, that what I worry about never happens, that I needed to apply the brakes and accept that God takes care of things.

I like to think of myself as self-sufficient, as being able to fend for myself. These last few days I had a dose of loneliness. I was keen to get moving and I knew no one with sufficient English to discuss my feelings. How I welcomed the family's replies to my emails. Jacinta and Angela had been giving me much encouragement. Jacinta was keen to tell me of the various people she had been meeting back home who marvelled at what I was doing – a seventy-eight-year-old father who was walking across Europe. These ruminations ceased abruptly when Gemma dragged me out of myself and forced me to participate in the class. I was sad to sit in the classroom for the last time, yet keen to be walking again.

I enjoyed my last visit to the bar Media Luna. As I sat in the warm afternoon, I imagined that I was getting a good taste of the Spanish weather, ambiance and lassitude. The morning's anxiety vanished and I was relaxed, ready for tomorrow's adventure.

Back at Jacinto and Loli's, I packed a box I bought at the Post Office (*correo*). I was determined to lighten my backpack. The weight was 6.2 kilograms. That included items (clothing, books) I had bought in Pamplona but I reckon half that weight had been in my backpack.

After quitting the post office, I put my Spanish to the test by inquiring about a flower shop. I was told of two. I had in mind to buy Loli a thank you gift. At one of the shops I discussed my needs with the shopkeeper. I was hoping she spoke English, but no, we had to discuss my purchase in Spanish. I selected a small orchid in a pot. It turned out to be a perfect choice for Loli because she had a table at the end of the dining room covered with orchids in pots. My gift fitted in perfectly. Strange, I had dined in that room every evening for two weeks and had never consciously noted the table although I was very aware of her beautiful antique furniture. Did I note the orchids subconsciously and had that perception guided my choice?

14. It's not the places you visit but the people you meet

I t was sad to leave Jacinto and Loli. They packed me a lunch to send me on my way. Early in the morning I walked through the Parque de la Media Luna, past my favourite bar, the Plaza de Toros, the Plaza del Castillo, through the familiar streets where mechanical sweepers were cleaning up yesterday's rubbish, through extensive parklands, all the time following the shell symbol and yellow arrow.

Other pilgrims were afoot early, and groups of cyclists, following the same line of shells and arrows. We greeted each other with *Buen Camino*. Otherwise the streets were quiet apart from an early tour group, the tour leader showing the way, and a group of elderly Spanish dressed in white and wearing red scarfs, preparing for a festival. In a few hours the street would be full of tourists on what was going to be a hot day.

It took an hour to clear Pamplona to continue my odyssey of wandering across the north of Spain. I felt the Camino enclosing me once more as I began the slow, tough climb to Alto del Perdon. All the other walkers passed me on the ascent, but I passed a walker whom I could see was in trouble. She was overweight, sunburnt, had a number of plastic bags full of stuff hanging from her pack and grasping more in the hands, at the same time holding on to her sticks, and was wearing light sandals.

I greeted her in Spanish and she replied in English. She said she was from Russia and asked me how far it was. I'm not sure what she was referring to, but I replied that you had to get to

145

the top of the hill and then it was downhill. We walked for a while. She was perspiring freely in the Spanish sun. Like me, she had started that morning at Pamplona and was hoping to get to Santiago. I doubted whether she would make the Alto de Perdon. I offered to carry some bags but she said she would sit down to rest and then rearrange her things. I offered her some of my sun block cream but she said she had her own. I wished her well.

I thought about that Russian lady all day, how unfit and unprepared she was for such a tough walk. Perhaps I could have helped her more, but then apart from my words of encouragement, I was not sure what I could have done. I could have offered her water but a plastic water bottle was among her accruements. I hoped that she would recognise that she was not ready and return to Pamplona. The Camino can be cruel for the ill-prepared.

The road became steeper and the track rougher. Pamplona lay in the valley behind me. Many walkers and cyclists passed me but eventually I reached the Alto de Perdon, a small plateau with a line of cast iron cut out sculptures of pilgrims on foot and horseback, plus two donkeys and a dog. My Spanish was good enough to read the inscription:

Donde se cruza el camino del viento con el de las estrellas

(Where the path of the wind passes that of the stars).

I could look out in all directions, back to Pamplona and ahead to Puente la Reina, like viewing a map displaying where I was, where I'd been and the country still to come. Then began the descent. Just as rough. I was alone for a while but then groups of cyclists rattled past. I reached the bottom, stopped to sit on a large rock and ate the lunch Loli had prepared. The cyclists continued to pass. One iridescently-clad young man slid in the loose stones and came a cropper in front of me. I sprang up to help, but he was on his feet, on his bike and on the way. I was surprised he suffered no consequences from what seemed a bad fall. Was he sore later?

I kept meeting the same people all the day. I spoke first in Spanish. Thanks to Pamplona I had learned sufficient vocabulary and a repertoire of simple phrases to handle the normal daily exchanges. I'd like to think the Spanish recognised that I was speaking their language in Spain, that I was making an effort to communicate, even if my accent was atrocious.

Everyone asked your destination and where you started. Some were out for the day or the weekend. Many started at Pamplona and were planning to walk to Logroño or Burgos, before returning to work. Only a handful was aiming for Santiago. My destination that day was Puente la Reina but as I passed through Obanos about two kilometres short of the larger town, I thought both the *albergue* and the village seemed nice places to pause. Twenty kilometres was enough for my first day back.

The *albergue* consisted of one dormitory of thirty-six beds and was memorable for its courtyard with a large fig tree. Under that fig tree I met Eric. Up to then I heard German and the speakers were content to talk with each other. Eric spoke to me in French. He was French and had set out from Paris via Tours to walk to Santiago. He had walked for a while with an Australian who had taught him some Australian, such as *G'day, No Worries* and *It's your shout, mate!* He told me that, being French, food was important to him and he liked to dine well each night. He invited me to have dinner with him, so we adjourned to an adjacent restaurant and were seated at a table with a number of Germans. They didn't know French and not much English. It's amazing how a meal can relax people. Plenty of food shared around a common table creates family. Eric liked his red wine and so did the Germans, so we had a good night. I slept well despite the number of roommates.

Obanos is the place where the *Camino Aragones* joins the *Camino Francés* and both continue on to Santiago. Known as *La Voie d'Arles* or the *Via Tolosana* in France, it commences at Arles and continues through Montpellier and Toulouse before crossing the Pyrenees into Spain. It was the route used by pilgrims coming from Italy. The pilgrim routes from the north of France had already joined the *Via Podiensis* before Saint-Jean-Pied-de-Port, so all roads lead to Santiago. The pilgrims from the north and east of Europe had been funnelled into the *Camino Francés*, a reason why I could expect a greater number of walkers than in France.

I started early and soon reached Puente la Reina (Queen's bridge). I walked along the main street, lined with a succession of grand houses, small palaces and churches, until I reached the bridge which gives the town its name. The town was quiet. The pilgrims who stayed there the night had already left. The bridge is beautifully restored. I paused for a while to admire the symmetry of the structure as it straddled the river.

I walked with a young teacher from England. Aaron was tall, wearing a beard, floral shorts and sandals. He was interested in me as an Australian and why I had come so far. He was also interested in my age. I replied that I had dedicated the Camino to the memory of my wife. Suddenly I thought of a new motivation. The Camino was a celebration of life. I was offering thanks for health and for my fitness which allowed me to undertake such an arduous and demanding project.

Before I commenced walking I was worried whether I had

the tenacity to persist day after day with such a demanding physical and emotional task. I know that I have tenacity as I started the previous year at Le Puy and had already walked close to 900 kilometres, including the stretch from Saint-Jean-Pied-de-Port to Pamplona. I was planning to reach Santiago, still another 600 kilometres.

Aaron had started at Pamplona and was aiming to go as far as he could before the end of the month when he had to return to work. We stopped for a break in the middle of an arched medieval bridge and met a young Italian Salvatore and two German girls.

Other walkers – including the Germans who shared our dinner table the previous night – were bathing their feet in the river. The group of us walked along a stretch of Roman road to a small village (Cirauqui) where we stopped again, squatted together like a tribe at rest and shared our food.

I shared my peaches and gave Aaron some antiseptic for his blisters. I asked Aaron and the others why they were walking the Camino. They found 'the reason' hard to put into words. They disguised their discomfort with banter. The idea grabbed them and captured their imagination, they said. It was something important to do. Something they always wanted to do. Other than that there wasn't much more that they could say.

I had heard this kind of answer in France and I was sure I would continue to hear it in Spain. In fact, I felt the pull myself like the forces of gravity. I just had to come back. Most of the young people who were walking belonged to a generation where institutional religion was irrelevant to their lives. They had no awareness of a belief that the purpose of life is union with a Divine reality. They'd been told that the purpose of life was to get a degree, make money, have kids and die. Yet, they respond to spiritual signals. They are seeking a spirituality to live by.

They are responding perhaps to something greater than themselves. In previous times pilgrims knew what they were doing and why. A pilgrimage was a way of atoning for sins and doing penance, of asking a favour of God or a saint, or fulfilling a solemn promise. Most of today's pilgrims know little of this style of language. They just feel pulled. Yet they know about sharing food, about attending to each other's blisters, of encouraging each other to get going when they can't go any longer.

Salvatore asked me to write in his autograph book. Quaint because I thought autograph books had died out a generation or two ago. Not so. The book was his way, he said, of keeping a record of the people he met. I could not think of anything original, so I wrote an old cliché. *'It's not the places you visit but the people you meet.'*

The day was memorable for the Roman road and number of roman and medieval bridges we crossed. I reached Lorca after about sixteen kilometres where some walkers stopped at the *albergue*. The village was having a fiesta and all the inhabitants seemed to be lunching together along the main street. They were dressed in white and wore scarfs and bandanas. Some were red and others were blue as if they were in different teams. I decided to walk to the next village Villatuerta but they were having a fiesta too and the *albergue* was closed. It seemed the people running the *albergue* didn't want caring for pilgrims to interfere with their fun. I was tired and disappointed. The village people were dressed in white, red scarfs and bandana and were sitting down to a meal together in the main street. Every village it seemed was having a fiesta for the weekend. That made sense as Monday 15th, being the Feast of the Assumption, was a public holiday. Everyone was making the most of a long weekend.

At the end of the street, I recognised the Germans from the

previous night sitting at a trestle table in a large open shed. *Come and have some soup,* they beckoned. On another table were a number of large soup tureens. The shed looked as if the village's communal meal had been prepared there. At the rear was a row of burners and gas bottles. The organiser had invited the passing pilgrims to share in the left overs. So I sat down to a bowl of soup and a glass of red wine and drank to the health of these generous villagers who had reached out to care for the passing pilgrims just as their ancestors had shared their food and wine with the pilgrims of old. In my time in Spain I was gaining the impression that wine for the Spaniard is what beer is to the Australian, one of the natural joys of living, and should be shared. I could have spent the rest of the afternoon in the shade of that shed.

The nourishment gave me the strength to walk the extra five kilometres to Estella where, although they were having their own fiesta, the *albergue* was open. I was tired, having walked twenty-seven kilometres and I was surprised at the attitude of the *hospitalero*. He spoke to me in French. I had met Eric in the queue and he may have heard us speaking. He was snappy and annoyed when he asked for my passport and I had to dig for it right at the bottom of my pack.

I had heard that the opinion of many Spanish people towards the French is still marked by mistrust mainly for historical reasons. Emperor Charlemagne sacked Pamplona in the 800s. Then, France's second emperor Napoleon the First reduced other Spanish towns to dust. Invading French armies have given the Spanish a bad time.

Perhaps my *hospitalero*, who was in his sixties, may have dealt in his younger days with French tourists who had a reputation for arrogance and disrespect towards their poorer neighbours. Such memories would have upset his Spanish pride and he was transferring his mistrust, albeit mistakenly, on me. Even after my passport revealed my true allegiance, he was still cranky. Poor bloke, the *albergue* was large and full. With the many demands of his guests, he became anxious and flustered, almost to the verge of a nervous breakdown.

Eric and I dined together at a local restaurant along with an Italian couple from Sardinia. After dinner, I was sitting in the courtyard waiting for the sun to set before going to bed. There I met my first Australians. Others had mentioned meeting a father and daughter team so I was hoping to meet them sometime. I was told he had a white beard. So when I saw an older man fitting the description I spoke to him, this time in English. I was delighted to hear an Aussie accent. He lived out of Hobart. His daughter arrived. She was studying in Melbourne. They had both visited London to see a family member and then came on to Spain. She could only spend a few days with her father before returning to London, but he intended to walk to Santiago. However, he was pressed for time and was planning to catch the bus across the Meseta. How often had I heard that story! Pilgrims had given themselves a certain amount of time but it never seemed enough. They had no time to pause. They had work to return to. They had to rush, walking thirty kilometres plus a day, or bus across the less interesting sections. I was thankful I had the time to appreciate the Camino deeply.

We had to be out of the *albergue* by 7.00 am. I said goodbye to Eric who was planning to push ahead because of his limited time. Two kilometres after Estella was the village of Irache, the site of one of the first Benedictine monasteries in Navarre, famous in medieval times for its pilgrim hostel.

More interesting was a bodega opposite where the vintner had installed a *fuente del vino* (wine fountain) with two taps, one for water and one for wine, offering pilgrims some wine to strengthen themselves for the way ahead. The inscription read:

Peregrino! Si quieres llegar a Santiago con fuerza y vitalidad, de esta gran vino echa un trago y brinda por la Felicidad.

(Pilgrim! If you want to reach Santiago strong and healthy, have a drink of this fine wine and raise a toast to happiness.)

Although the water flowed freely, the wine tap was dry. Perhaps 7.30 am was too early for a drink.

We had a tough climb to Villamayor de Monjardin and I welcomed the opportunity for a good rest. Just as well I had not pressed on to this town the previous night because the *albergue* was closed for the fiesta.

I noticed a group of Spanish pilgrims. Among them was a dog wearing his own small backpack. I walked through Los Arcos, along a very long main street (Calle Mayor) crossed the river and found their albergue. It was open and the Belgian *hospitalera* was warm and welcoming. She spoke in French.

I liked the *albergue*, a number of buildings around a large courtyard. A hot day with a breeze made the courtyard an ideal place for drying washing. How important these little benefits were! I was ever hopeful that by the time I had stopped for the evening I would have enough time for a shower, a siesta, to wash my sweaty clothes and for them to dry before nightfall so that I could pack my backpack in readiness for a quick departure in the morning. Life was reduced to simple needs.

Salvatore was in the bed opposite. He thanked me for my entry in his autograph book. He thought it was the best entry he had received. I was pleased because I thought it was a cliché but he recognised it as truth. I suppose many clichés contain the truth. That's why they are written so often. He told me he had stopped last night late at Villameyer and because the *albergue* was closed he had to sleep in the handball court with about fifteen others. I remembered that handball court because I had paused for a drink at the adjacent bar. The court was a stretch of partly sheltered concrete. What a hard bed that surface would be!

Unlike the French *gîtes* , the Spanish *albergues* accepted no reservations. First come, first served. Not a problem if you stopped early enough before the full sign (*completo*) appeared. Not having to make reservations avoided the need to plan ahead. You had no real objective. You stopped when you felt tired. In other words, you lived for the day, for the moment.

The fiesta at Los Acos was in full swing. About 6.00 pm the pilgrims crossed back over the bridge and joined the townsfolk, all dressed in white with red scarfs, for the running of the bulls.

The young men took up their vantage points around the main plaza and street, the little old ladies were on balconies, the older men were in bars barricaded with steel posts and the youth were on the fountain. I found a space on the church steps and later crossed the street during a lull to a barricaded bar.

The bulls were released in threes or fours and scrambled through the plaza and down the main street and back again to the enclosure. The local youth jumped off the fountain and ran across their path. The bulls menaced their tormentors and the onlookers yelled encouragement from the safety of their vantage points. Whether they were encouraging the bulls or the youth I wasn't sure.

The procedure was repeated for an hour. Otherwise it became boring and I must say frankly I was pleased when they stopped the bulls and removed the barricades.

The crowd adjourned to the arena where once again the

local youth teased the bulls. I felt sorry for the poor creatures. I was waiting for the excitement, for something to happen, for, say, a professional toreador to emerge dressed in his costume and put on a show. Nothing happened.

After an hour they removed the bulls and the people focused on the bars and the fiesta stalls. Unless I had missed the finer points, I could not see much point in bull-running. I found it far more entertaining to saunter invisibly along the street with its many bars, the people sitting outside, chatting, joking, shouting, singing, eating, drinking, playing guitars, thoroughly absorbed in enjoying their fiesta to notice me.

I suddenly found myself wishing for a face I knew, so I returned to the *albergue*. I slept well although in the distance I could hear the rumble of a disco across the bridge in the town.

I left the *albergue* before 7.00 am while it was still dark. I enjoyed my first two hours of walking in the cool morning, a time for solitude and reflection. As the sun rose, I could feel that it was going to be a hot day. I stopped for breakfast at the little hilltop village of Sansol. In the bar the television presenter was giving the weather forecast. His map showed a string of forty degrees around Spain. It was going to be a hot, hot day.

At the next little village about a kilometre away, (Torres del Rio) I came across the group of Spaniards among whose members was the dog with backpack. He had become a favourite of the road and responded to the attention that everyone gave him. Someone threw him a stick and he enjoyed the game, dashing back and forth across the plaza while the human pilgrims rested in the shade.

I had intended to walk to Logroño but with the rising temperature, my body was telling me to go easy. Viana was eleven kilometres, Logroño another nine. I decided on Viana. I was applying one of the vital lessons of the Camino: *Don't push yourself too far or take on too much. You'll regret the exhaustion and dehydration.*

Much of the day was spent walking through a dry, brown, stony land interspersed with vineyards and olive groves. The heat radiated from the ground below and the fierce sun bore down from a cloudless sky. The light was as lethal as the heat. The country was stark and harsh, yet beautiful.

After six hours I arrived at Viana. The main street was crowded with people taking their lunch. There was no room to pass by the many chairs outside the line of bars and restaurants. Outside the ornate church (Santa Maria), where the storks roosting in the tower gazed solemnly across the town, I met Salvatore. I missed him in the morning. He told me he had been locked out because he arrived back after the curfew. He was enjoying himself at the fiesta and stayed longer than he intended. Salvatore slept on the lawn in the adjacent park. Despite two nights in the open, he was bright and cheerful. The extravagance of youth! He left me to charm two slim, fair haired, attractive German pilgrims who would stir any male's blood.

The *albergue* stands out because it was the only one I stayed at with triple bunks. My room was small with three sets of bunks. What little room that remained was taken up by a set of lockers. It had no windows, only one opposite the door in the corridor which overlooked a narrow laneway.

Despite the heat which built up during the afternoon, I was grateful to be inside away from the forty degrees plus as I lay down on my bunk (a bottom bunk) for my siesta. I was grateful, too, for the lockers which gave me a place for my backpack.

In contrast, the *albergue* had a spacious dining room and kitchen, but I decided to eat outside. In the laneway, there was the dog with the backpack, but this time his backpack was removed and he was tied to a drain pipe. I found a restaurant with the pilgrims' menu. In medieval times, pilgrims got by on bread and wine, but today, pilgrim's menus offered three courses of plain food – usually a soup or salad, a choice of three or four mains, and a dessert of ice cream or yoghurt. No gourmet meals in Spain! A meal cost eight euros, a bed five euros, so you could live cheaply. I walked around the town before returning to the *albergue*. The dog had gone.

In a corner of the dining room I found the diary. Every *albergue* has one and you are invited to make an entry. I looked at previous entries. I was amused by a page which a budding artist had filled with sketches depicting the dire consequences of sleeping in triple bunks. A long way to fall from the top! An entry in English from the previous week grabbed me. A mother had endured a difficult day and dedicated the hard walk to the memory of her son who had died of suicide earlier in the year. My heart went out to that lady. I could feel the pain she was suffering. My heart goes out to everyone bereaved by the suicide of a loved one. Our suffering binds us together and even though I will never meet the lady who wrote the diary entry, our common pain makes us brother and sister. We are pilgrims on a journey. I thought of my Maris. I thought of the suffering she had endured. I thought of my own sense of loss and hollowness. I felt the tears threatening to overflow. I wrote an entry addressed to those pilgrims who were walking the Camino following some tragic loss and hoped that the Camino would give them the strength to endure their anguish and continue with their lives.

I became aware that the group of people sitting at the other end of the table were looking at me. I was sad, crying inside but I didn't think I was weeping openly. They were the group of Spanish walkers whom I had seen earlier that day. One of them spoke to me. In English she was apologising that their chatter might be distracting me. On the contrary, I replied. I was merely writing in the *albergue*'s diary and had finished. She invited me to join them.

Her name was Mercedes and everyone (ten of them) introduced themselves. Mercedes asked about my background and she translated to the others. I was grateful for the opportunity to chat, as if this friendly mob of Spaniards had been sent at the right moment. I mentioned the dog with the backpack and Mercedes explained he belonged to Anna, one of the group. Through Mercedes, I asked Anna where her dog was. His name was Patum. She explained that, at first the *hospitaleros* would not allow her to bring the dog inside so she had to tie him up in the laneway, but as night fell, they said she could put him in the room where the cyclists stored their bicycles. We spent the next half hour chatting. They said goodbye because they were finishing the next day. Back in my room every bed was taken. My roommates were Spanish cyclists who by now had shed their lycra and were lying naked on their beds.

After a hot and airless night, the first stirring was at 5.30 am. The cyclists slipped on their lycra and departed. I left by 6.30 am.

I enjoyed the dark cool of the morning, on my own and moving at my own pace. Early morning was a time for reflection and for prayer, one of thanks for the day and for my health. There was no conversation with others who passed me, no more than *Hola* or *Buen Camino*.

As I was constantly walking west, the sun rose behind me. My shadow stretched way ahead. I could see the advancing shadows of walkers about to pass me. I would hear the tapping of their sticks first. Then they drew level and passed on. This morning was different. All the early risers had passed me and it would be a little time before the second wave caught up. I was alone. All I heard was the sound of my own feet hitting the road. Yet I sensed a presence. Someone was walking with me. I felt close to that Presence. I almost expected another shadow to appear beside mine. Then as the sun rose higher and my shadow shortened the Presence seemed to depart, but I was inspired by the experience as if God or Jesus or even Maris were supporting me for a brief moment on my lonely road. I was enthused, brimming with confidence and ready to walk forever.

15. The voice that calls me, I hear at the deepest part of me

That morning, Wednesday 17th August, I left the autonomous region of Navarre and passed into la Rioja, famous for its wines. I was making good progress across Spain. I may have been excruciatingly slow to some but I was getting there. I walked with Julia, an unemployed social worker from Germany. She hoped the Camino would help guide her future direction.

Many local people seemed to be just as consumed with the Camino as the pilgrims. I came across one such person on the road leading into Logroño. She was an old lady who had set up a stall on the roadside and offered to by-passers water and her stamp for their *credencials*. *Credencials* are usually stamped at the *gîtes* and *albergues*, but along the length of the Camino many cafes, bars, and churches have designed their own distinctive stamps and are very willing to stamp the pilgrims' *credencials*. This old lady spent the entire day, every day, stamping *credencials*. Her stamp depicts her name (Felisa), the town name Logroño, some figs, a pitcher of water, a cross along with the inscription *higos, agua y amos* (figs, water and love). She gives out a cheerful greeting and figs when in season from the tree overhead.

I arrived mid-morning at Logroño, a large town with a cathedral and other churches. I visited the church of Santiago. Outside it had an equestrian statue of *Santiago Matamores* (St James the Moor Slayer). Legend has it that in the time that the Moors occupied the Iberian Peninsula the people prayed to St James to get rid of them. The Moors were defeated and expelled and it was reported and believed that St James was in the battle and fought with a drawn sword at the head of the Spanish troops on horseback.

A statue of St James as a pilgrim was inside. St James depicted as the moor slayer wasn't right. St James as the gentle pilgrim was more in keeping with my image of the compassionate nature of an apostle of Christ. Here was the first church in Spain offering facilities for candle lighting. Under a larger than life tableau of Christ dragging his cross I lit two candles, one for Maris and one for Joe, and sat in front of them gazing at the flame. The candles represented my suffering, my grief and the pain of loss. They reminded me of the depth of my love. They represented the courage to confront my sorrow and to face the changes in my life. They recalled the times we cried and laughed together. I lit those candles so that the light of Maris and Joe will always shine.

It took a long time to pass through Logroño. The way marker arrows and shells were difficult to locate but eventually I found my way to the edge of town to a park with a long promenade between the hills and wetlands.

The locals were walking, running, cycling and they outnumbered the pilgrims.

I had lunch with Emmie. She was from California and lived in Ireland. I had heard her American accent a number of times. When I introduced myself, she told me I was famous. Other pilgrims had spoken to her about meeting a nice seventy-eight-year-old Australian walking solo. I was one of the interesting characters. Perhaps it was because I greeted others in a variety of languages to get the right one. Her story told me how gossipy the Camino was. Everyone talked about everyone else, but not in a malicious sense. The talk was caring. If someone was flagging or having a tough time, people cared for them. People would say to me, 'I haven't seen so and so today. Have you seen him?' I might say, 'No' or perhaps 'Yes, I talked to him outside the bar at the last village. He's okay, just having a breather.'

I stopped at Navarre. The *hospitalero* at the *albergue*, who was very warm and welcoming, told me that a fiesta was happening. I watched the running of the bulls for a time but, becoming bored, tried the bar by the *albergue*.

I met a group of six pilgrims who were walking together – five Italians and one Spaniard. Juan was the only Spaniard, Frederica the only woman. The other Italians were Roberto, Dario, Emiliano and Stephano. They warmly included me in their group. Emiliano was an architect; he would love to visit Australia and practice his profession. Dario's girlfriend of eight years wanted a baby. He was not sure and was walking the Camino to help him decide. Frederica was a masseuse. She wanted to massage my back that night.

We ate a meal of pasta together in the *albergue's* spacious kitchen. The camaraderie of the Camino! The wine flowed and we had a great night together before retiring to the noise of the fiesta outside. The night was hot but I went to sleep quickly but was woken at 1.00 am by the first blast of a disco just outside the window. I had noticed them without suspicion setting up the equipment in the plaza in front of our bar.

I doubt if any pilgrim slept that night. A disco offers no relief. The machine that plays the music needs no rest. It's relentless, in contrast to a live band which has to have a spell once in a while. Added to the racket was the operator's raucous gravel voice which broke in too frequently and grated nerves already jangled by the ceaseless music. He had a limited repertoire for he repeated the same tunes, or was it because disco music is so tuneless that you can't tell the difference? I got up early as there seemed no point in suffering any longer. I usually offer thanks for the fact I've alive for another day but was there anything to be thankful for that morning?

As I packed my bag and climbed down the stair, I felt much the same as I do after a harrowing overnight shift with Lifeline. The bleary eyed *hospitalero* looked as though he had as much sleep as his pilgrims. He repeated his apologies. Outside, the disco was in its dying moments. Young male bodies were staggering or lounging over tables, empty bottles and cigarette packs were strewn everywhere, the savage smell of stale alcohol hit the nostrils.

A relief to get out of the town, away from the glare into the cool, dark morning. Navarre replaced Montcuq as the arse end town. My thoughts about the Spanish were not charitable. No wonder their economy is in a parlous state. They spend all their time partying. I was beginning to liken Spain to visiting a crazy family in a perpetual state of mania.

I was tired but as I immersed myself in the rhythm of walking, I seemed to regain my breath. I longed for a cup of coffee and was grateful for the first bar. My friends from the night before were already seated. We compared notes. No one slept. Efforts to block out the noise, like ear plugs or covering one's head with a pillow, were fruitless. Frederica complained that she had heard one song five times. Some variety would have been bearable. But spirits were high and the group departed cheerfully to leave me to finish my coffee.

I was always intrigued by the graffiti along the Camino and usually stopped to read them. Written in a variety of languages, they were the creations of earlier pilgrims who had taken the trouble to write on walls, fences, footpaths, stones and fences. The walls of pedestrian underpasses were usually rich in content. They had many messages. That day, I photographed *Semper Fidelis* (ever trusting) and *J'ai mal aux pieds* (my feet hurt). On the approach to Najera, someone had written in beautiful script on a concrete retaining wall a poem by a priest, Eugenio Garibay Banos, first in German and further on in its original Spanish.

My English version doesn't match the beauty of the original:

The Way
Dust, mud, sun and rain,
it's the pilgrim's road to Santiago.
Millions of pilgrims
for more than a thousand years.

Pilgrim! Who calls you?
What hidden force leads you?
Neither the way of the stars,
nor the grand cathedrals.

It's no longer the bravery of Navarra,
nor the wines of la Rioja,
nor the seafood of Galicia,
nor the fields of Castile.

Pilgrim! Who calls you?
What hidden force leads you?
Neither the people on the way,
nor the country customs.

Neither history nor culture,
neither the cock of Calzada
nor the Gaudi palace,
nor the castle of Ponferrada.

I see all in passing
and it is a joy to see all.
But the voice which calls me,
I hear at the deepest part of me.

The force which pushes me,
the force which leads me,
I don't know how to explain it:
Only He Who's above knows.

I paused to read the Spanish and translated it ever so slowly. The Spanish word *arriba* means 'above'. I had already read the French version in my *Guide Spirituel du Pèlerin,* which I bought in France the previous year. *Celui d'En Haut.* He who is on high is the English translation. I have been asking myself the question every day, particularly as the going gets tough: why am I doing this? What's pushing me on? Why did I start last year, go home and come back this year to continue to Santiago? He who is above knows, he who is on high. A force far, far stronger than me, calling from the deepest part of me, giving me a craving, an addiction to persist. The gravitational pull towards Santiago had gripped me like a vice. It wasn't me pushing my body along the route. It was Santiago dragging me forward.

Najera, like so many places along the Camino, has a substantial history. In the 10th century, when Pamplona fell to the Moors, the Christian king transferred his seat to Najera. Originally part of Navarre, it was absorbed into Castile. I passed through the town and continued on to Azofra where the *albergue* was excellent. No sign of any bunk beds; accommodation consisted of two-bed cubicles. Luxury! Sharing a room with one person! Other luxuries included a spacious kitchen and a large courtyard with pool. Such ideal places for chatting, for getting to know the other pilgrims, for dangling feet in the water, for building community. I was now evaluating *albergues* on the opportunity they offered for intermingling.

Sometimes, communal areas were hopeless. There was no kitchen, only pokey dining areas, no courtyard or other common area. My roommate was Emiliano. His friends called him Emi, he said. I was pleased he had invited me to use his nickname, a sign of acceptance. I was always conscious of my age difference with my fellow pilgrims, (Emi was twenty-nine) but always it didn't matter. Not once was I patronised or made to feel an old bloke.

All my friends from last night were there. Like a family reunion! We had a few drinks and a meal together. Frederica was keen to have her photo taken with me several times. Amid much jocularity and laughter, the boys were suggesting she had the hots for me. They were not the words they used, but that was the intent. Another great evening made it easy to forget the physical demands and hardships of the day.

Back in our room, Emi and I chatted. With his thirtieth birthday approaching, he saw himself at a crossroads. He liked his profession of architecture but was more interested in creating modern buildings rather than restoring ancient monuments. He liked Spanish schools of architecture. Were there opportunities beyond his native Italy? After the deprivation of the previous night, I slept very soundly.

Emi had departed when I woke. The sun was just rising as I passed through the *Albergue*'s gates. Up to now, the way had been dry and dusty, but heavy rain overnight made the track fresh and muddy. It was a change to find mud rather than dust clinging to my boots. The morning freshness was a miracle of renewal, but the signs were that of a hot day ahead.

A steady flow of walkers passed me. Most were friendly,

greeting me or responding to my greeting, but some were silent, either ignoring me or grunting. I accepted that many knew no other language than their own and were reluctant to enter into any conversation however brief. But others were withdrawn and the wall they had built around themselves was almost visible. I left such people to themselves but they were a challenge and I was curious about their motivation. Were they carrying a burden so crushing that they had to look inwards constantly? Were they trying to survive a severe loss? Or was the answer simple – shy folk who had never been happy with their communication skills, or contemplative souls who had come to the Camino for solitude, not for chatter?

I passed Frederica and her friends several times. Nothing shy or introverted about them! They were constantly laughing and joking with each other. I would find them resting by a fountain or outside a bar. I'd join them and then they would move on. I walked with them briefly but I invited them to move ahead because my pace was too slow.

Coming across Ciruena was bizarre. At first I skirted the boundary of a golf course, then passed an elaborate golf club building and a subdivision of new roads and villas. Apart from a few cars outside the golf club, there were no people. No one was playing golf.

The villas and apartment houses were empty, their gardens were choked with weeds. The weeds in the nature strips flowed over the footpath and road. This brand new village was deserted. A ghost town! Usually ghost towns are derelict and decayed, relics of former good times. I'd seen some deserted villages on the way; the buildings, possibly hundreds of years old, were crumbling away. Their good times were past long ago, but here in this special purpose town, the good times never arrived. What was the development destined to be? A retirement village? A suburb for Burgos? Now, it was a sample of Spain's economic woes.

The countryside is dotted with ghost towns, huge housing developments unfinished and unsold. I had already passed several of these building sites where nothing was happening. A Dutchman told me there were 735,000 apartments for sale in Spain. Imagine the human cost in a country where the value of housing fell by up to fifty per cent, leaving many owing mortgages worth more than the property involved, where in up to 1.7 million households no one was working, where the government does not expect unemployment to fall below twenty-two per cent for several years, where 10.5 million (equal to twenty-five per cent of the population) are considered to be on the edge of poverty. Poor Spain!

I stopped for two hours in Santo Domingo de la Calzada. I visited the cathedral of San Salvador and its museum. The most unusual feature was a cage with live poultry high up one of the inside walls, reminder of a miracle. I've heard a number of versions of the Tale of the Cock and the Hen and the following is one of them:

A family with three pilgrims stayed in an inn in the town. The innkeeper's daughter is said to have made advances to the son, but he refused the offer. In revenge she secretly placed a bag of money in his baggage, and the following morning discovered that the money was missing. The family was pursued, the son was bought before the judge and condemned to death. The parents continued their pilgrimage to Santiago, but on the return journey, spent the night in San Domingo de la Calzada once again. The mother was not convinced that her son was dead. She went to the place he had been put to death and found him there, alive, though still hanging. Accordingly, the parents went to the judge and asked for their son to be released. The judge, who was sitting at dinner, refused to believe them. He declared the boy was no more likely to be alive than the cock and hen on his table. He told them to get up and fly- which they immediately did, proof of the son's innocence.

Probably no one takes the tale seriously, but it's a satisfying story and an important part of the town's folklore, a medieval legend that has endured down the centuries. The symbol of a cock and a hen features in the town's emblems and the cathedral's *credencial* stamp.

Back on the job, I pressed on to Granon and found the parish *albergue*, attached to the church. A medieval building had undergone a renovation of sorts. Entry was by an ancient spiral staircase. There were no beds, just mattresses on the floor and they squeezed in about fifty people – primitive but the community feeling was great. A meal was included free as was the mattress. Donations were accepted.

The young *hospitaleros* were warm and welcoming, and the pilgrims were respectful and good humoured. No one seemed to care about the old mattresses or the cramped conditions. What was more important was the caring attitude of the *hospitaleros*. To the pilgrim hospitality and welcome count, appearance is not important. That is another lesson of the Camino which I hope to carry back to my real world. A glossy exterior is nothing if compassion and kindness are missing.

Many of my friends on the road were among the guests, including Frederica and her mates. I spoke for a time with a Norwegian lad on the mattress adjacent to me. I learned from him a lot about Norwegian life and culture. He had become bored witless in his bank job, resigned and had decided to walk the Camino. When he returned home, he wanted to be a nurse.

An older Swiss recognised my accent and told me he had spent a year in the 70s in Sydney learning English. Sadly, he was one of the very few on the Camino who got on my nerves. He told me a joke about the Aussie accent. The sound *ay* as in *day* can sound to non-Australians like *ie* as in *die*. An Australian visitor to Shanghai concerned his hosts when he told them he 'had come to China today'. What annoyed me was hearing him repeat the same story to other groups. I was tempted to ask him had he learned in his English lessons the phrase 'You give me the shits!' I had to avoid him in case I succumbed to my temptation.

Granon had its fiesta, too. After dinner, I wandered to the town plaza on the other side of the church where a stage had been erected and a live band was playing popular Spanish music. The balmy night was ideal for dancing. All the locals were dancing. Only the very old seated on the low walls and steps of the fountain were watching. The rest – couples, families, young children were swaying to the music. The pilgrims joined them. Frederica grabbed me and we danced together, her friends on the sidelines yelling words of encouragement. I was hoping the musicians would stop at the latest by midnight to allow us some sleep, but they were replaced by a disco which blasted all night. Fortunately, the solid church building muffled the sound and, although troublesome enough, the music was nowhere near as loud and intense.

The disco was still going when I left the *albergue* and could still be heard over a kilometre away. I walked with my Norwegian neighbour to Castildelgado where we shared breakfast. I met Frederica and her friends. You feel so close to people sometimes. When you see them you feel you've known them for years but it's only a few days. They had to push on to Burgos as they were due back at work the following week. It was sad to say goodbye and after many hugs I watched the six of them walking abreast down the road until they disappeared. I was grateful for their welcoming me into their boisterous company but now I was conscious of being alone again.

The Spanish heat was intense. On the outskirts of Belorado I came across a small park. An older local had wisely taken cover. As he occupied the only seat in the shade I asked if I could join him. My limited use of his language encouraged him to talk to me. I could not understand but that didn't bother him. He continued his monologue. I said the occasional *Si* and nodded, and that spurred him on with more information. Perhaps he just needed to talk to someone and I happened to come along. I wondered what he was telling me. A story of many years ago? A grievance with a neighbour? How the younger generation is going to the dogs?

He asked me where I was from, and the answer seemed to impress him. I understood his asking me where I was staying that night. I said in Belorado. He said that the *albergue* just along the road was good. In fact, he got up with me and walked with me in the heat to the *albergue*, pointed up the drive, wished me *Buen Camino, Peregrino* and walked back to his seat. I found it hard not to eulogise on this simple gesture towards an unknown pilgrim, insignificant in the weighty struggle between good and evil, but simple acts of generosity like this old chap's tip the balance towards good. There is hope for us humans, yet.

The exterior of the *albergue* was inviting. The path to the entrance was lined with national flags. The municipal *albergue* and town centre was about a kilometre further on. It was time to stop and accept the old chap's recommendation. The

modern purpose built *albergue* offered single room accommodation but I was happy with a five euro bed in a dormitory.
After the routine of checking in, washing oneself and the day's
clothes, I enjoyed a siesta, thankful that I had stopped early for
the temperature was approaching forty degrees. I had a drink
and dinner with an Irishman. Danny, like so many of the other
walkers, was exhausted from the heat. I probably was more
heat tolerant than most but I took precautions, drinking plenty
of water and giving myself a relatively easy day (seventeen
kilometres).

In the morning I indulged myself. The early risers were long
gone by the time I stirred. I had decided on an easy day and
would walk twelve kilometres to Villafranca. I could afford to
leave late. I was pleased with the decision as the Spanish sun
heated the land very quickly. The main memory of the walk
was a fountain at Espinosa del Camino where I ducked my
head under the tap. What did it matter if I got myself wet? I
would dry out in no time.

At the fountain I met Georg and his girlfriend Veronika.
Getting to meet people on the Camino is a matter of chance
or coincidence, but later it seems as if there was design in
the encounter. At first the other pilgrims seem like one big
crowd but then individuals begin to stand out. I first noticed
Georg the previous Sunday because he was wearing a ring on
his lower lip. He joined us pilgrims, just as I was leaving, at
Villatuerta where the locals had invited us to finish the soup
and wine left from their fiesta. I had noticed him at other
times on the way and wondered if the ring interfered with
eating or drinking. Dunking our heads together gave us the
first opportunity for a chat. Veronika and he were students
from Dresden in Germany. They were planning to walk the
full distance to Santiago. We walked together, the three of us,

to Villafranca. (Town of the Franks). They, too, decided it was too hot to go any further.

The *hospitalera* was welcoming and told me she had another Australian in the house. The combination of the heat and fatigue made it an ideal afternoon to lie low and I slept for three hours, my longest siesta so far. I met the other Australian. Adam was from St Kilda in Melbourne. His wife and he had commenced the Camino at Saint Etienne, but she broke her ankle on the first day. She returned to their daughter in London but he decided to continue. Adam had no Spanish and hadn't bothered to learn even a few survival phrases. He seemed unskilled in communication and I had a feeling he had isolated himself. He was only speaking because I was a fellow Australian. Perhaps he was one of those fellows whose wife does all the talking. If he had said he had made his Camino a silent retreat I would have understood. I felt sorry for him for what he seemed to be missing out. *It's the people you meet not the places you visit.* For me, the opportunity to meet so many people is one of the Camino's blessings. As part of your inner spiritual journey, you are able to recognise and respect the interconnectedness of all people.

I walked through the town looking for a restaurant, but bought some food at the bar-cum-supermarket to prepare a meal back at the *albergue.* The kitchen and dining area were under cover in a yard at the back. There were Georg, Veronika and a number of others. Georg greeted me warmly and introduced me to the others. In no time I knew everyone. That's the Camino's way. You make a friend, you meet his friends and they become your friends. How grateful I was to have decided to return to the *albergue* rather than eat alone, as if Someone up There on High had determined I should eat in company.

I had seen Michael previously. He stood out from the crowd

because he had only one arm. He was Danish and walking alone. Ed and Clare were English. By day Ed was a policeman and she was a teacher of handicapped children, but at night they were professional singers specialising in folk songs. A mixture of Spanish, Italian and Dutch made up the remainder of the party.

We pooled our food together and people were given jobs. Clare was the organiser. Teaching handicapped children turned out to be an excellent background for organising such a cosmopolitan mob. We had a delicious meal of salad and pasta, lots of it, topped off by a dessert of fruit, and plenty of red wine. Everyone produced a bottle. Then Clare and Ed led the singing.

After a number of English folk songs, we had to sing national songs. Each song called up another. My contribution was Waltzing Matilda, and everyone including the non-English speakers joined in the chorus. As the sun set and darkness descended, the *hospitalera* came out and asked us to quieten down because they were putting the old people to bed in the nursing home next door. I thanked Ed and Clare for a wonderful evening. I thought of Adam as I crept past his bunk. What a great night he missed. Once more I thanked He Who is on High for leading me to this group.

A steep climb out of Villafranca led me into a pine forest. The road was muddy and the smell of pine cleared the lungs, freshened the morning darkness, and made the steep incline easy. There were no other walkers. As always I valued the morning silence and the solitude. I valued the sense of having a forest around me after having walked through cleared land for days. The light mist added an air of mystery.

According to my guidebook, this was an area to be avoided at night in former times because of the hazard of wolves. I was grateful the dangers facing the medieval pilgrim are no longer with us and the Camino is actually a safe place. The terrain flattened out and I could both hear and see the main national road coming closer until I was just above it. At the high point before the descent was a crude monument with an inscription in Spanish.

I have roughly translated:

Monte de la Pedraja 1936. In this place were executed three hundred persons who supported the coup-d'état of General Franco against the legitimately established republic and which gave rise to the Spanish Civil War between the years 1936 and 1939. They were assassinated in the first years of the civil war for their political ideals and for defending liberty. This humble monument, erected by their families will ensure that we will never forget their memory.

I paused by this simple monument. I looked around; an isolated place off the road between Logroño and Burgos. A perfect place for a mass execution. Up to now the emphasis of the Camino had been on medieval times. My guidebook mentioned many places where once was situated a church or hospital for pilgrims. Many churches boasted a 12th century origin. I also came across monuments commemorating a conflict during the Napoleonic wars. Here was a monument recalling a tragedy in my lifetime, one of many atrocities committed by both sides in a civil war notable for the passion and political division it inspired.

A lot of digging had taken place in the scrub behind the monument. I walked among the ditches. They were excavation trenches. It's hard to describe the eerie feeling which wrapped me. The place was spooky. The mountain was silent – no wind, no birds, the day was dull, the sky overcast. The ghosts of this mass execution were hovering. Four pilgrims hurried by.

I was curious enough about this site to do some research. I looked up Monte de la Pedraja on the internet at the next opportunity. Following the executions, people from Villafranca had been forced to dig the graves and the incident traumatised the town for many years with no one daring to speak until ten years ago. They had begun excavating in 2008 and by early 2011 had discovered 104 bodies but had difficulty in identifying them as the victims came from all parts of Spain. I guess there is still more excavating to do.

As I descended the mountain I brooded over this monument. This was my closest encounter with the Spanish Civil War. What unhealed scars remain? I thought of the many massacres and mass executions that had taken place around Europe during the Second World War and after. From time to time the media reports the discovery of a burial pit and the evidence points to a mass execution. Such events seemed remote, of fleeting interest, but here I was in the mountains that had contained the dead for so long, the massacre was so close. Real people with wives and children; sons and brothers had been killed. What kind of lives did they lead and whom did they leave behind? I may have walked over bodies yet to be exhumed.

My mood was sombre. Human beings are capable of terrible atrocities. My heart was heavier than my pack. I needed to lift my mood, to turn my thoughts away from death. As I reached the plain the mist lifted. The sky cleared and the sun shone brilliantly on a vast field of sunflowers. I had seen many fields both in France and in Spain. The flowers I had seen so far were mature and ready for harvesting. The heads were too heavy to lift and the leaves and stalks were straggly, but the rolling hills before me were covered in neat rows of young sunflowers stretching from the edge of the road out to the horizon. The stalks were erect and the heads were held high, as if they were proud of just being.

Sunflowers are flowers with faces. Their dark seedy central disk surrounded by a collar of yellow petals make them happy, hopeful faces. As their French name, *tournesol*, and the Spanish name *girasol* implies, these faces follow the sun, itself the source of life. They can't get enough and even before the first beam of light has peeked over the horizon, their faces are pointing east, ready to soak up the first ray. As the sun rises, these flowers follow. They trace its ascent and descent, gradually turning towards the west until the day is gone and the last light has faded away. By dawn they are on the ready again and facing east when the sun rises. How do they do it? I haven't a clue. I can only say that it is such a graceful and simple movement that you forget your own pain and fatigue in wondering at one of God's mysteries.

More amazing is the way these flowers move as one. Since they are sowed in orderly lines, their fresh yellow rimmed faces line up in ranks, row after row, extending to the horizon. What's more, all these flowers are pointing the same way at the same time. They are like bright happy children in rows lifting their faces together in silent tribute and hope.

No doubt the farmers who sowed these flowers wanted the oil in their seeds, but to me, they had another value. I've always admired sunflowers as a symbol of hope. The sunflower dies but it produces new life in the thousand or more seeds in the central disk. I have used the sunflower as a symbol in my work at Lifeline facilitating groups for people bereaved by suicide but here on the Camino they sowed hope in my heart, particularly on days I was so tired I wondered why on Earth I was here.

Now as I left the site of the massacre behind me, they lifted my mood with their message of hope, that out of these dark tragedies one can begin again.

My pleasure and sense of delight was great, almost joy. My pack was so light that I forgot I was wearing one. It was one of the special moments of my pilgrimage. I thanked God. My mood had done a ninety per cent swing. Life had replaced death. Hope had displaced despair. Those sunflowers touched a core value in me. I believe deeply that even in the worst of situations, if there is some hope, there is the possibility of life and recovery. In my work supporting the bereaved by suicide, I witness how a sense of hope can inspire people to cope with their trauma and continue on with their lives. I felt reinforced that what I was doing for the bereaved was right and I resolved that, when I returned to Sydney after I reached Santiago, I would continue.

In the middle of the sunflower fields was a tiny village. San Juan de Ortego boasted a restored large pilgrim church and monastery. I lingered in the cool depths of the church, clean and bare, full of wide and curving spaces, established by the saint San Juan de Ortego as a shelter. Not only were the mountains infested by wolves in medieval times, they were also overrun by bandits. I found Georg and Veronika resting outside the bar, ready to depart. Being too early to stop for the night, I followed them and pushed on to Atapuerta. Atapuerta is famous for its archaeological excavations which made a spectacular find: the fossilised prehistoric 'Atapuerta man'.

I found my friends from the night before installed at the *albergue*. Once again, we shared a great evening – Ed, Clare, Michael, Georg, Veronika, two Spanish couples. Our communal meal was followed by a range of singing and music, everyone contributing a song from their country. I was called

on for a repeat of Waltzing Matilda. Our singing was contagious and soon everyone joined us.

The ladies of Atapuerta had set up breakfast, so in the morning the pilgrims, as they left the *albergue*, crossed the road to
the community centre where coffee, hot chocolate and food
were provided. The ladies were a wonderful example of the
way the locals along the Camino care for their pilgrims. They
enjoyed their job, were pleased by the gratitude of their guests
and seemed delighted in having their photographs taken. I,
too, was thankful and, if my Spanish were better, I would have
asked them if this was a one-off or did they provide breakfast
every morning.

Fortified by my hot chocolate I climbed the sharp incline
out of the town and soon found myself on asphalt on which I
spent most of the day walking. Instead of allowing my mind
to drift, I tried meditating to the sound of my foot beats on
the hard surface. My walking with its constant rhythm and
forward motion became a prayer. Just being there walking was
a prayer. No need for special intentions, agendas or plans on
what to or not to do or what to pray for.

At one time I tried saying a decade or two of the Rosary
each day. The repetition of the Our Father and Hail Mary
was in itself a mantra, but I could see that it wasn't necessary.
Walking was sufficient. Let me stay with the moment and the
movement, let what might happen happen, let the Camino
teach me.

I found myself walking through nine kilometres of industrial zone at Burgos. The hours could have been dreary but
I amused myself by guessing the business of each of the
enterprises lining the road. Some were easy, particularly if
they listed their products on signs at the front of the building. Others had me guessing as they listed products not in my

vocabulary. The area was strangely quiet. I had visited industrial zones before and they were bedlam with their traffic and operating machinery. Here in Burgos many of the factories seemed closed with a handful of vehicles in the car parks. Traffic was light, with only a few heavy trucks. The one factory which seemed fully operational was a huge tyre factory identifiable by the smell of rubber.

Was I seeing another indication of the wretched state of the Spanish economy? Factory buildings gave way to commercial buildings and shopping plazas. I arrived at the *albergue*, a six storey renovated building in the older part of town, with an ancient façade and modern interior.

I was allocated a bottom bunk in a four bed cubicle on the third floor. The dining area with its long wooden tables and benches was large enough but the kitchen had no facilities for cooking. The *hospitaleros* were friendly and welcoming but this vast *albergue* had no soul. I found my friends of the last two nights scattered through the various levels of the building but as we could not cook and dine together our little community was lost, swamped in the hubbub of a busy city. We had to work our ways through the throng of tourists and find our own dinners in the multitude of bars and restaurants.

16. No man is an island

My guidebook suggested that Burgos was a place to spend at least a whole day. The capital of Castille, it has a gothic cathedral and many other important buildings. Sadly, they compete with an uncontrolled urbanisation. After one night in the traffic, crowds and racket of a big city, it was like a gulp of spring water to return to the open countryside. The morning was cool and the way was through a few kilometres of suburbs with grand houses. I fell in with two Irish ladies without backpacks, who greeted me warmly.

I asked them how long had they been walking.

One replied, 'Ten minutes.'

Therese and Catherine had started that morning and were planning to walk to Léon. They were to have their baggage transported. I met these ladies a number of times during the day. I met Georg and Veronika. They, too, did not like Burgos. They, too, ached to be back in the rustling silence and solitude of the quiet landscape. It was as if we been released from the constraints of a prison and able to roll free.

I commenced walking across the Meseta, a broad plain that stretched out before me for the next 250 kilometres. Many find the Meseta boring and take the bus. I did not find it dull. I valued the time. Even though I was walking for a large part through stubble fields I was relaxed and content. At one stage I prayed that I would make Santiago and that I had the strength to push on. But as I walked I felt as if I was being pulled along, that the forces of the Camino had taken over and were propelling me in a steady rhythm along the track. As I mentally felt over my body, my legs were holding up and my feet were without blisters. At one stage I thought reaching Santiago was possible but now I felt it was inevitable, as if the steady act of walking had mesmerised my spirit and body. What really pleased me was that the pain in the muscles in my back which I experienced in France was absent. My 'off season' efforts had paid off.

I arrived at Hornillos del Camino about 1.00 pm. It's a one street one bar town. My guidebook described it as a small village with a large gothic church, formerly an important pilgrim halt with a hospital and small Benedictine monastery. The word *hornillo* means 'little stove', so perhaps it was also important for its hot food.

It was a good place to halt for the modern pilgrim. In fact, it struck me as an ideal village after the chaos of Burgos. The contrast couldn't be greater. No bright lights and masses of tourists trawling the bars. The *albergue* was already full but they placed the overflow in the *mairie* (local government office) and in the gymnasium at the local school.

I got my five-euro bed with eleven others at the *mairie* along with Georg and Veronika. They had made friends with the others and in no time I was their friend, too. In the afternoon I lay on my bottom bunk bed, intent on a siesta, but chatted to Georg instead. I liked Georg. He bubbled with youthful enthusiasm. He and Veronika knew each other at university. He was studying mathematics. They were walking the Camino for spiritual reasons and to get to know each other. He was interested in the Catholic faith and liked many of its practices but was unlikely to convert because his parents were Lutheran ministers.

Among my roommates was another couple, Jacob and Elena. She was Dutch and he was German but they conversed in

English. They had met on their first day of walking at Saint-Jean-Pied-de-Port and decided to walk together. They were still walking together and stayed in the same *albergue* each night. They had become an item, a Camino romance.

In the story in the Acts of the Apostles the disciples on the road to Emmaus met Jesus. I wondered if I might meet Jesus. Not that he would be wearing long robes or a beard. It could be anyone, young or old, male or female, but the encounter could have some special significance. I had met two possibilities in France.

That afternoon, I met him. He was sitting on the steps of the large gothic church next to the *albergue* soaking his feet in a dish of hot water. He told me he was Spanish, from Madrid, and had started walking that morning at Burgos although he had travelled the Camino many times before. Hence his feet were tender and sore. He spoke broken English with a slap-dash gusto. He was intrigued that I had come so far. I was intrigued that his name was Jesus. Jesus is a common name among the Spanish.

The pilgrims had spilled out of the crowded albergue and spread themselves over the steps of the church and the adjacent plaza. There were Ed and Clair, Michael, and my other Spanish friends from previous nights. Michael introduced me to Don, a Canadian, and to Sheila, an Australian. She came from Sydney, too. She began at Pamplona. Her husband walked with her for a few days but had to return to work in Australia and she continued.

My two Irish ladies strolled by. Theresa and Catherine were staying in Hornillos, too, but not at the *albergue*. They had chosen the *casa rural*, a kind of hotel, at forty-five euros a room, and had their luggage delivered. Don was staying there, too. He didn't want to risk having his sleep disturbed. A group of young Spaniards were in the plaza, talking only to themselves. They did everything loudly. I was happy they were in the main *albergue* and not in the *mairie*.

The Meseta has its own beauty. It was majestic to climb to the top of a rise and see the path stretch out before you for kilometres across an arid shallow valley through brown fields to a mystical distance. No trees. The fields were covered with stubble as if a cereal crop had not long been harvested.

Step by step I made my way across to the next rise to be greeted by a similar view. Besides me, other pilgrims were moving between horizons. We often remained in sight of each other, gradually gaining or losing ground until they eventually moved ahead.

I was fortunate to strike fine weather for in this featureless landscape, seemingly devoid of human habitation, one could be at the mercy of a harsh sun, fierce winds and storms with no one and nowhere to turn to for relief or shelter. I enjoyed the silence, the solitude and the vastness. It made me realise my place in the world. I was just a tiny dot and it wouldn't make much difference whether I was here or not. Nevertheless, I was part of it, part of God's creation. I thought of the beautiful lush countryside of France when I had to stop and gaze in wonder at the green hills and valleys. I had the same awe. The landscape was stark but just as magnificent. Who said the Meseta was boring?

I found that one of the great benefits of the Camino was to be alone and content with my thoughts. Mostly, my mind was in neutral and I did not think about anything, just content with the rhythm of my road. The movement of my legs and feet was my prayer, a voiceless tribute of thanks. It was like being semi-conscious or in a coma.

Every now and then my mind left my body to walk on the

path, jumped into gear and engaged itself with some matter related to my life back in Australia – what improvements are needed for my new home, whether I should buy a new car on my return. Random memories sprang into life and they led from one to another. My mind wondered down the bypaths and back roads of my memory.

I thought of many incidents, sometimes with pleasure and other times with shame. It seems much easier to remember the hurts, the failures and rejections. It seems more common to gather our life energy around a hurt than a joy. Always there were reflections on my life with Maris, on the many incidents and events we shared in raising our family.

These memories led on to sadness and regret that she was not with me. Could I have done more to keep her in this world? I had to remind myself of the many joyful times in our forty-two years of marriage. Memory is the basis for both pain and rejoicing. We don't seem to have one without the other. Together they map the course of a journey towards new insights and new hopes, an interior pilgrimage that matches the exterior physical quest. A passing pilgrim, flowers by the roadside, a twinge of pain in the thighs, a sudden realisation that I was hot and sweaty brought me back to the present world and I was walking the Camino.

I stopped at Hontanos and found Jesus sitting outside a bar. He seemed very pleased to see me. In his mixture of Spanish and English he told me he was always getting lost, not only on the Camino but in life as well. I told him I would pray that he didn't get lost today and left him to finish his beer.

I continued on to Castrojeriz. The town is long and thin and shaped like a sausage as it curves around a hill dominated by the ruins of a castle. The area suffered in the 11th and 12th centuries as the wars between Christians and Saracens moved back and forth, soaking the ground with much Christian and Moslem blood. Imagine the depth of violence, the immense efforts to build the fortifications, the fierce determination of the attacking armies and the equally fierce and desperate resistance of the defenders.

Everything was peaceful as I entered the long, thin town. At the municipal *albergue*, Michael, Ed and Clare were sitting on the terrace. Michael said he was checking in his Camino family. The young people had already arrived. By that he meant Georg and Veronika, Jacob and Elena. They welcomed me as a family member and offered me lunch. The *hospitalera* was warm and welcoming. She had bunk beds for twenty-two and eight mattresses. I got the last mattress. Sheila had arrived just before me and was on the adjacent mattress.

That night I had dinner in a restaurant beautifully restored in a medieval ambience with Ed, Clare, Michael, Sheila and Don. We reminisced about the highlights of the brief time we had been together. Ed and Clare were saddened. They had to wrench themselves away from their Camino family as they were departing the next day for England, back to their jobs and their real world. I was saddened, too. I found them good company and each day I looked forward to seeing them in the evening.

I had told Clare some of my story and she had told Ed because he had already expressed his sympathy at my losing Maris by suicide. He had hoped that I would find happiness. They saw me, I think, a lost soul, adrift and searching for an anchorage. Perhaps they were right. Once again I said goodbye to friends. Letting go and starting over are part of the pilgrims' progress.

When we returned to the *albergue* the young people were sitting over the dinner, inevitably of pasta, sipping the last of their wine. Georg had enjoyed his wine and perhaps was feeling randy for he wished he was sleeping in a double bed that night. Veronika gave his hand a gentle slap. They were walking together, Georg told me, to get to know each other. As they shared the beauty and the burden of the Camino, I guessed they would want to come closer physically.

What people did about sex on the Camino I wasn't sure. Sexual encounters are hard to arrange in open dormitories. In my 'off season' back in Australia my daughter Angela, remembering her youth hosteling days, asked if I witnessed any 'bonking on the bunks'. I had to say no. No doubt if lovers were desperate enough they'd find a way, in the still of the night or in a field off the track.

On Friday morning I walked in the dark through the remains of the sausage-shaped town. Before me rose a fierce hill which climbed steeply out of the plain that housed Castrojeriz and its castle. The sun rose behind just as I topped the top of the hill and sent my shadow far ahead. A cold wind was blowing strongly and I wore my gortex most of the day. The terrain was flat and so the walking was easy.

I met Catherine and Therese a number of times and walked with them. They wanted to know something of me and my motivation. I told them I had walked across France last year and had started this year at Saint-Jean-Pied-de-Port. By the time I reached Santiago I would have walked 1500 kilometres.

I felt in a jocular mood so I cast humility aside and boasted that I had carried my backpack all the way and had spurned the services of the baggage carrying companies. I had also spurned the bus, had walked every step of the way and intended to complete the Camino on my feet.

Catherine described me as a hardcore pilgrim. I mentioned that hardcore pilgrims were inclined to look down on walkers without backpacks. They were tourist pilgrims, doing it the easy way. They were inclined to agree, perhaps condescendingly that I was taking the difficult option when there was an easier means available.

I tried to explain that although it might be a walking holiday for them I was on a pilgrimage and saw myself as a successor to the ancient pilgrim following the same route that millions had pursued before me. Those types had it tough facing physical dangers such as wolves and brigands and the medieval version of the conman and although the way was easier for the modern pilgrim there were still arduous challenges to be faced. Therese and Catherine were motherly types and were keen to order me around and tell me what to do. I was not to overdo things. I was to take care of myself. They were tourist pilgrims but they shared the same concern for the welfare of other pilgrims as the hardcore.

After a good day of flat walking I arrived at Fromista and found my Camino family at the *albergue*. There were Michael, Sheila, Georg and Veronika, Jacob and Elena. I was fond of the young ones, as Michael called them. They had a good command of English so communication was easy. In fact, they seemed to appreciate learning more English from my conversation. They had learned English from books at school, they told me: it was good to hear the vernacular, particularly the Australian idiom.

The noisy young Spaniards had found the *albergue*, too. They did everything loudly – talk, walk, sleep and fart. They showed little interest in talking to other pilgrims.

The *albergue* lacked a kitchen but dinner was available at one of the numerous restaurants. I dined with Michael, Sheila, a Dutch couple, a French lady named Eloise, and Don who, once again, had spurned the crowded *albergue* for a hotel room. Our

Camino family was flexible. People came and went but everyone was welcome. We were not building a permanent house on the Camino; our dwelling was only temporary, but while it lasted we enjoyed the camaraderie of each other's company.

The day was spent following a path which ran parallel to the road, like a cycling track – easy walking although less comfortable because of the traffic. I longed for a rural silence but had to listen to the thunder of passing trucks just a metre or two away, some with enough draft to dislodge my hat. I walked with Teresa and Catherine who continued to offer me advice. They stopped at Fromista, not in the *albergue*, but in a hotel, and, had their luggage transported.

Carrion de los Condes, according to my guidebook, used to be a large town of 12,000 inhabitants with twelve churches and several pilgrim hospitals. Now the population is 2800 and depends solely on the passing of pilgrims, not unlike many other towns and villages both in France and Spain.

In most of the *albergues*, conditions are crowded with pilgrims living on top of one another. The *albergue* at Carrion de los Condes was no exception. As usual, I managed to obtain a lower bunk but there was barely enough room to put down my backpack.

As always, people were respectful and tolerant although the noisy group of young Spaniards were in residence, just as loud as ever. Their behaviour was more obvious because they were so much the exception.

Among the pilgrims were my Camino family – Michael, Sheila, Georg, Veronika, Jacob and Elena.

We went to the church Santa-Maria del Camino for evening Mass. The young priest was very enthusiastic and gave a blessing to the pilgrims. He had developed a special service. I kept the booklet because it included the Lord's Prayer in a number of languages. I knew the prayer in English and French and was getting to know the Spanish version.

Back at the *albergue*, we sat down to a communal meal. Jacob prepared the main pasta dish. It was delicious and we praised him. He remarked that he was not used to praise. At home he had only received criticism from his father. If he had done well there was no comment. When challenged, his father's argument was that children need to get used to the rat race of the real world. We discussed the value of praise as a way of developing self-esteem. Despite the lack of praise from his father, Jacob seemed a competent and confident young man. I learned later he was an officer in the German army.

We gossiped about our fellow pilgrims. These northern Europeans found the noisy Spaniards just as annoying as I did. How wonderful it was to spend another evening in community, sharing our stories and journey together, gaining strength for the following day's rigours in our mutual support and trust. The cliché *No Man is an Island* applies to the Camino just as validly as to real life.

17. I'm searching for an answer that may never be discovered

Sunday morning's walk was rigorous. Between Carrion de los Condes and Calzadilla de la Ceuza lay a stretch of seventeen kilometres. A straight road was before us as we pilgrims set out for the day's walk. Usually one was able to purchase breakfast or a coffee early on but this day there was nothing, just a straight road with few trees to provide shade.

I ambled along at my usual pace and was amazed at the numbers that passed me. I looked down the straight road before me; I turned to look behind. There were hundreds. Talk about a crowded solitude! Where had all the people come from? Being a Sunday, many may have been walking just for the weekend or just started walking that day.

The sun was bearing down hard and I had the impression from body language and facial expressions that many were finding the going tough.

Hundreds of the lycra-clad cycled by. Their clothing was impressive with many colours and slogans. Their gear looked expensive. Some were in teams, their clothing like a uniform. Many couples were wearing identical outfits. Even their saddle bags mounted over the rear wheel were matching. They reminded me of the material world where pretence, illusion and appearance expensively purchased were important.

For the moment I had left that world view behind and opened the heart to the simple life and the simple routines.

At one stage I saw a vehicle driving slowly towards me through the walkers. The Spanish Red Cross was out for the day, ready to help any casualties. I was thankful that I was carrying plenty of water. I hoped I wouldn't need their help.

The road ran straight and flat. Eventually, it arrived at Calzadilla de la Cueza, a large name for such a small village. The bar was overflowing. Tired pilgrims filled the chairs and tables outside. Among them were Georg and Veronica. Georg was chirpy but Veronika was feeling very tired and they had decided to stop in the local *albergue*.

The Red Cross van came by. Out jumped four jovial workers who distributed balloons with the Red Cross emblem and joined the pilgrims for a drink. I grabbed a handful to take back home for the grandchildren.

I was weary myself and glad for a rest, but after a coca cola and some banter, I felt fit and keen to move on. The way was just as flat. Someone had written graffiti in English on a stone:

Being in the present.

The reminder was timely. I imagined exhausted pilgrims were wondering when would the day end, when would they find relief, when could they do something about their blisters. What you needed to do was to put one weary foot in front of the other, pace by pace, and eventually you'd arrive.

Shortly after I arrived at Terradillos de los Templarios, another tiny town with a big name. On the outskirts was a cafeteria/restaurant/bar/*albergue*/hotel. The building was modern, large and imposing and too new for a garden to be established on the very flat level piece of ground. The chairs and umbrellas were inviting, so I stopped. There were Theresa and Catherine enjoying a drink in the shade. The map on the reception wall indicated that I had walked 402 kilometres since Saint-Jean-Pied-de-Port, only 379 to Santiago.

The friendly *hospitalero* offered me a ten-bed dormitory for seven euros, a four dormitory for nine euros or a room for twenty-eight euros. I chose the ten-bed dormitory but I had only one roommate and he spent all of the time caring for his puffy feet. I joined Theresa and Catherine. They had walked the long road but, as usual, had their baggage transported. They were sharing a thirty-six euro room.

I was surprised at the small number of pilgrims staying the night, in sharp contrast to the numbers on the road and to other nights when the *albergues* had been full. Perhaps the complex was too new to be included in the guidebooks.

I had dinner with the Irish ladies. They were keen to know more about me and asked questions. In turn I enquired about their background. They had left their husbands back in Ireland. Neither of them was a walker. The ladies had only a day or two left of their holiday as they were returning to Dublin from Léon. As I went to bed I was grateful the noisy Spaniards had gone elsewhere.

My roommate's feet must have improved for he departed very early. The route ran parallel to the road and an endless row of trees planted about every ten metres provided islands of welcome shade. I thanked those officials who organised their planting many years ago. In some places the trees were too young to provide a shade and pilgrims years ahead would benefit from their foliage. For the moment, I was thankful for what shade was available.

I was intrigued that there were fewer walkers in contrast to last week. Perhaps for many the summer holidays were over and they were back at work. Others may have decided that the many days of flat walking was too monotonous and had taken the bus.

It was a welcome relief to greet the occasional pilgrim as they passed me. On the way, I came across Sheila, Theresa and Catherine, and Michael, all resting at a bar. After the small town of Sahagun the Camino divided, the two paths running more or less parallel with the railway line in between. One followed an old Roman road but had no shade for thirty kilometres and was isolated. The other continued the tree-lined route. I chose the shady path. Bercianos del Real Camino took twenty-four kilometres of easy walking.

The parish *albergue* was run by volunteers and a donation rather than a flat charge was expected. The *hospitalero*, an American from California, explained that the evening meal was communal and each pilgrim was expected to bring some food to be prepared by the volunteers. Rather than everyone bringing the same, each pilgrim was allocated a certain type of food. My contribution was a melon for dessert.

In the *albergue* I found Michael, Jacob and Elena. I walked with Michael to the shop to buy our contributions. The owner was named Jesus, so I can say I met Jesus for the second time.

The afternoon was hot so Michael and I enjoyed a couple of beers in a sun-bleached bar on the way back to the *albergue*. The communal meal was great. Many languages and nationalities were represented. The *hospitaleros* organised some singing. One of them had a guitar. My contribution was *Waltzing Matilda*, which went down well with the largely Spanish crowd. They wanted an encore. I even heard some of them singing the chorus later. At the rate I was going, I was waltzing with Matilda all the way across Spain.

As usual I left the *albergue* before dawn and in the dark had difficulty at the edge of town finding the correct way. I retraced my steps to check where the yellow arrows pointed. I saw a group take the path to the left and I followed them. The sun rose and I continued along the path, the group by now having disappeared ahead of me. After about forty minutes a car drove by and stopped. The driver spoke in Spanish but I understood that he was telling me I was on the wrong path.

'The Camino is over there,' he said, and pointed across the field.

In the distance I could see a line of trees which looked like a continuation of yesterday's shaded path. As confirmation, I could also discern the silhouette of a walker complete with backpack. I thanked my informant, who drove on. Another example of the care and concern the locals have for their vulnerable pilgrims.

I hope he catches up with the others, I prayed, as I made my way across the stubble.

Where did I go wrong? Where would I have finished? How long would it have taken me to discover my mistake? It was not the first, nor the last time that I had taken the wrong turn. Safely back on the Camino, I saw the group tracking across the stubble ahead of me. They reached the Camino just as I caught up with them. When he saw me, one of them sang *Waltzing Matilda*. Shortly afterward, another Spanish walker sang *Waltzing Matilda* as she passed. The Spanish were learning Australia's favourite song.

I always stopped to read the graffiti. On the back of a road sign someone had written in English: *In the house of my father there are many rooms.* Further along the same hand had scribbled: *It's not about churches. It's about him.*

Among the pilgrims I found a few churchgoers, but many told me they hadn't been to church for years. Yet there was a spiritual motivation behind their journey. They were somehow seeking the divine but not through any church.

There were a number of pedestrian tunnels which took the

walking track under the road. Their walls provided plenty of space for statements.

On 14.8.2008 an anonymous author had defined peace in English:

> Peace: It does not mean to be in a place with no noise, trouble or hard work. It means to be in the midst of those things and still be calm in your heart.

Next to this piece of philosophy Esther had written on 16.8.2011, also in English.

I'm searching.
Finding an answer
so deep that it maybe
will never be discovered
hoping and praying
that my life has a light
forgiven past and future
road to paradise.
Wandering and seeking
may you find
whatever you seek
as a burning light in the dark
that shines brightly in the deep
as ghosts
haunting the mind
precious memories that you once left behind
may you find
and be
open the heart
and be free.

Esther has described the search which so many pilgrims including myself had embarked on. Another message dated 8.4.2010 told passers-by that *It was a long road from death to birth!* and *Thanks to all pilgrims.*

Was that message a reflection on the writer's journey? Perhaps the Camino rejuvenated their life and brought them back from the brink. In the same group was a reflection written in French. A rough translation follows:

There will never be enough kilometres to rid all the anger.
There will never be enough kilometres to reach your ideal.
But there will always be enough to understand that love and mutual dependence are more important than all.

I stopped at Mansilla de las Mulas for the night. The *albergue* was built around a courtyard hanging with freshly watered flowers, the baskets still dripping. Everyone congregated in the cool, an ideal communal area.

Jesus was sitting at one of the tables. He seemed pleased to see me. He thought I was the best and wanted to have his photo taken with me.

Michael was staying too and I had dinner with him and Don, the Canadian and Catherine the French lady. Michael had all the gossip. He seemed to spend a lot of his time talking to other pilgrims and they were happy to tell their story. No doubt he told others about the Australian just as I told others about the Dane with one arm.

The night was disturbed. By now, I had learned to avoid bunks too near the exit sign lights but this exit sign light was as bright as the ordinary light. In addition, when I went to bed there were three empty top bunks. In the half-light someone arrived late and tried the three beds before settling down.

After a restless night I was tired, dragging the chain and felt the need for an early coffee. Approaching Puente Villarente I noticed a bar at the side of the road. Bars were usually readily identifiable. Chairs and tables were outside, a number of backpacks lying around and the sound of music emerged from an external loudspeaker. This bar was different. Instead of the usual Spanish pop songs, the loudspeaker was playing Beethoven's 9th Symphony, 4th movement. Inside a number of CDs were displayed on the counter, all Beethoven or Schubert.

Just as I sat down outside with my coffee, the music changed with the run up to *Ode to Joy*. First I heard the melody, then a few bars of anticipation. On came the baritone and then the chorus. What an extraordinary moment! I immersed myself fully in the music and let it flow over me. I stayed until the end of the movement. I felt renewed, invigorated, and full of joy. I shed my tiredness, and felt more than ready to face the day. What a brilliant way to send me on my journey.

I met my two Irish ladies, Theresa and Catherine, on their last day. They planned to spend two days in Léon before flying to Ireland. They had enjoyed their holiday, they said. I was reluctant to call them pilgrims. To me they had done the Camino the easy way. They were not sure whether they would return to advance closer to Santiago. They wished me well and hoped I would make it. To the end Theresa was full of advice on how I should manage my life. There was only one lady whose advice I willingly accepted, and that was Maris.

I had read warnings about the approach to Léon, hazardous because of major highways. How many pilgrims were lost trying to cross such busy roads? I found an elaborate system of walk overs. The crossing was no longer a danger, just noisy from the roar of traffic. The pedestrian bridges were another indication of the money that had been spent on the infrastructure of the Camino. It took a while to walk through Léon, a large town with important monuments dating back to the 12th century.

I had the choice of two *albergues*. I chose the municipal *albergue* which doubled as a youth hostel. It was impersonal. The young *hospitalero* did not even look at me as he booked me into the computer. There was no kitchen and no communal area. None of my Camino friends was there. They stayed at the other *albergue*, a *monasterio* run by nuns. I did a quick tour of the town but after the quiet of the countryside, I felt swamped and disoriented.

I met a young Australian lounging outside the gate to the hostel. He had dark curly hair and wore a scarf around his head which made him look like either a revolutionary or a Caribbean pirate. We chatted as I, too, sat on the low concrete wall.

Alphonse told me he was born in Italy and was raised in South Australia. He was a vagabond, he said, drifting here and there as the whim might take him. His address was the Camino. He seemed to be living in the present. He was a charming likable rogue with a carefree spirit and I wondered what personal events led him in his early thirties to this life of irresponsibility when others of his age are concentrating on a career and/or raising a family. Another lost soul? He was a devotee of the Dali Lama and quoted a story.

When the Dali Lama was asked what surprised him most about humanity, he answered:

Man. Because he sacrifices his health in order to make money. And then he is so anxious about the future that he does not enjoy the present; the result being that he does not live in the present or the future; he lives as if he is never going to die, and then dies having never really lived.

I felt lonely as I went looking for a suitable place for dinner. I dined alone and missed the company of my fellow pilgrims. I was isolated. My pilgrim identity was lost, swamped in the crowds of a busy city. I was just one of the tourists.

18. Being in the present

Rain fell heavily during the night but had stopped by the time I set out.

Léon was getting ready for the work day.

Under a dull sky the streets were full of commuters advancing like an army towards the city. I found myself walking against the tide. What a contrast was the appearance of these townsfolk! Ranks of men in suits! Women with smart coats and umbrellas!

Once upon a time, I wore a suit every day to work and took care to be well-presented, clean shaven, and well-groomed. That morning I was in my baggy shorts and floppy hat, unshaven, needing a hair trim, clad in boots and backpack, shell dangling from the back – rough around the edges to say the least.

The people stared ahead, ignoring the solitary pilgrim but a few looked at me closely as if I were a strange feral creature sauntering through their midst. Perhaps they were envious. They were fettered to a career and hurrying towards a competitive rat race world while this sauntering old chap had tossed away the chains.

As I cleared the town and was walking through an industrial area, rain began to fall, lightly at first but after an hour a downpour made conditions difficult. The path ran along the N120, a very busy road indeed so in addition to the rain and mud, the pilgrim had to contend with the roar of traffic in the wet. The industrial area continued for about ten kilometres, the view of factory after factory uninspiring. Rain and the thunder of heavy trucks made this day the Camino at its worst.

At least these Spanish trucks did not have trailers, unlike their Australian counterparts which too often tow a trailer as big as the truck itself. I had hoped to find solitude on the Camino, but not here!

I met the item couple, Jacob and Elena. Still together, they were walking separately during the day, Jacob being the faster walker, but caught up with each other at bars and for lunch and stayed at the same *albergue* each night.

I walked with Elena for a time while Jacob went ahead. Whereas Jacob was quiet, Elena was the opposite and ready to reveal her emotions and thoughts. I felt like a grandfather listening to the confidences of a granddaughter. She discussed her relationship with Jacob, whether it would endure beyond the Camino. When she commenced the Camino she had intended to walk alone but things changed when she met Jacob on the first day. He was the strong silent type, self-contained and self-sufficient. I imagined those qualities would have served him well as an army officer. It would be nice to think that their relationship continued after the Camino, like a holiday romance that blossomed into permanence. Elena left me to catch up with Jacob.

At Hospital de Orbigo, I crossed the longest bridge in Spain. I joined Jesus for coffee at a bar on the edge of town. We walked together and met up with Jacob and Elena. We took lots of photos of each other – the Spaniard, the German, the Dutch girl and the old Australian.

I liked Hospital with its quaint narrow streets and over-hanging balconies but it was too early to stop. Fortunately the Camino left the road and the path wandered across open country. How peaceful it was to be away from that road! I seemed to have been walking along or by asphalt and traffic for days.

I walked with Elena. She told me how often she had cried on

the Camino both from physical and mental exhaustion. She, too, did not like walking along a road. She moved ahead to catch up with Jacob.

There were plenty of walkers. Carmen spoke a little English. I had seen her a number of times without speaking to her, but she knew me as the older Australian who was walking on his own. She wanted her photo taken with me and her Spanish friends. So did another group who were French. People seemed to know me. The Camino is a gossipy place. I met Michael. We walked together for a time and shared our food for lunch. I had fruit and cheese and Michael had bread.

We looked around the spot that had enticed us to stop, and were saddened. It was a cool place, just off the track, shaded by overhanging trees that invited every passer-by to pause. It was strewn with plastic water bottles, food wrappings, drink cans, tissues, and even items of clothing such as handkerchiefs and socks.

A disappointing aspect of the Camino was the amount of rubbish discarded along the way, always in pleasant surround-ings – a shady spot, an excellent view – that enticed walkers to rest, not so much in France but definitely in Spain. Our lunch spot was one of the worst – a desecration of creation. I would have thought that pilgrims would have been sufficiently in touch with the natural world to take their rubbish with them. Sadly, many walkers had not learned the lesson of the Camino to leave nothing behind but their footprints.

As soon as I saw Astorga I knew I would like it. The Roman walls are visible and the excavations of a Roman villa are oppo-site the *albergue*. The *hospitaleros* were warm and friendly as they processed the steady stream of pilgrims.

I was curious about the number of disabled people riding in wheelchairs around the plaza. The *hospitaleros* couldn't explain their presence because they had no English and my Spanish wasn't up to framing the right questions. I assumed there was a hospice nearby.

I explored the town and liked what I saw. A series of plazas connect the town. I admired the clock on the façade of the Town Hall. Two pilgrims tell the time. As well there was the cathedral and the bishop's palace.

I found a bar in the middle of a park at the rear of the *albergue*. As I sat with my beer, I noticed one of the disabled in a wheelchair by one of the tables. He had very limited mobility and no speech. The waitress emerged from the bar, searched his bag, found his purse, took out some money, returned to the bar and bought back a beer which she placed on his tray. She put the change back in the purse and returned the purse to his bag. She took out a packet of cigarettes, placed a cigarette in his mouth and lit it. I was engrossed. He was barely able to take the cigarette out of his mouth and I wondered how he would drink his beer. I didn't wait. I felt a voyeur but I was touched deeply by the waitress' care.

He may have been a regular and she was carrying out a well-practised routine. Nevertheless, the incident struck a chord deep within me. We could regard their condition as hopeless, a twisted joke, but, as a society and as individuals, we need to reach out to the weak and disabled and care for them.

Every day on the Camino I thanked God for my health and fitness but I was extra grateful that evening for skills that I took for granted, such as walking up to a bar, ordering a beer, taking the money out of my wallet, checking the change, taking my glass with a steady hand, returning to my seat and drinking without spilling. What were simple routine skills to me was a daily challenge to this chap. I do hope he enjoyed his cigarette and beer.

Witnessing this struggle was one of my moments on the

Camino. I was subdued as I had dinner with Michael and Jacques that evening. I admired Michael greatly for the manner in which he had adapted to one arm. He sought help from no one and was able to go through the routines of packing and unpacking his backpack each night. I was humbled at how deftly he extracted the cork from a wine bottle and all those other tasks that normally require two hands. No fumbling.

As I lay in bed that night my mind wandered over my body. Everything was intact. I had fine coordination and the ability to think. I had so many gifts whilst others have few. Earlier in my career I worked with an organisation that trained handicapped people in social skills to fit them into the normal workplace. I formed the opinion that everyone – no matter how disabled and limited – has something to contribute. I prayed that I would use my gifts well for the betterment of others.

I missed Michael in the morning. My early walk out of Astorga through the three connecting plazas confirmed that it was one of my favourite towns on the Camino. I expected to see more pilgrims as many people start walking at Astorga. Furthermore, the Via de la Plata coming from Seville joins the Camino Francés here.

Along the way I met Jesus along with Carmen and her friends. The path took to the hills and running alongside it for a time was a wire fence into which previous pilgrims had intertwined crosses made from sticks, many hundreds even thousands of them. I had in my pocket the remains of wooden rosary beads which had fallen apart soon after I commenced the Camino and I had decided not to discard them but to wait for a suitable opportunity. This fence with its crosses was the occasion.

At Rabinal del Camino I found the *Albergue Gaucelmo* run by the Confraternity of St James. Gaucelmo was a fitting name because he was a 12th century local hermit who built a church, hospital and hospice for pilgrims. His spirit lives on because I received one of the warmest welcomes from the three *hospitaleros*, a husband and wife from Denver and a chap from Liverpool in England. The Confraternity of St James organises a roster of *hospitaleros* from its members, the wife was telling me. Volunteers stay for about two weeks. Everyone at some stage has walked the Camino.

The *albergue* had the remains of an orchard attached. The trees were loaded with fruit. I was offered a piece of Apple Crumble made by the *hospitaleros*.

Adjacent to the *albergue* was a Benedictine monastery, offering to pilgrims an opportunity for silence and prayer. You were expected to stay a minimum of two nights and join in their community life. The mission of the monks was to attend to the spiritual needs of pilgrims. In the church opposite they sang 'Lauds Vespers' and 'Compline' all in Gregorian chant.

Among the large crowd at Vespers I saw Michael, Jacques, Jesus, Carmen and other familiar faces. They were staying at the other *albergue*. Michael, Jacques and I had dinner together. The restaurant was boisterous and rowdy with conversations across tables in various languages, a good place to spend a Saturday night on the Camino.

The *hospitaleros* gave us breakfast and we were given a warm farewell in contrast to the cold morning outside. In misty rain and a cool wind we encountered a stiff steep climb out of the town and up the mountain. After about six kilometres, Foncebadon emerged out of the mist. It was an eerie sensation to walk through this almost abandoned village, looking as if some giant had knocked the pieces about and might at any moment return to scatter them, a wasted place on the edge of nowhere. The village has known better days judging by the number of ruined houses and crumbling walls and now seemed forgotten by the world. The mist added to the sense of isolation, abandonment and mystery.

About two kilometres on I arrived at the *Cruz de Ferro*. The Cross of Iron is one of the high points of the Camino. Its tall iron cross is built on a huge cairn. The heap of stones that has been built is believed to have been started by the Celts and continued by the Romans, which makes it the most ancient monument of the Camino. This very pagan monument was Christianised in the 12th century when pilgrimages were at their height by Guecelmo through the raising of a cross.

Traditionally pilgrims brought a stone with them from their home to add to the pile. The stones represented their sins. I had heard of the tradition and had brought four pebbles with me from Sydney. Just before I left I attended a Taizé church service where pebbles were used to mark out a pathway leading to a cross. I asked permission to take four. I had carried them all the way. I had planned to leave the four at the Cruz del Ferro but decided to keep one to throw into the sea at Finisterre.

I climbed the cairn and placed the three, one in memory of Maris and one for Joe and one for my bad points which I wanted to change and leave behind, such as being too judgmental. The occasion required a moment of reflection and prayer. I regarded the Cruz as a sacred place.

The steep climb made me hungry so I ate my lunch in a shelter by the cross. I met Jerry, an Irishman, who had started walking at Astorga. Then began the long descent and as morning merged into afternoon the mist cleared and out came the sun and warmth.

I passed through Manjarin, another almost abandoned village with a Spartan *refugio*, until I came to El Acebo, a village with a single long narrow street whose old houses have overhanging balconies and outside staircases leading up to the first floor.

I found the *albergue* at the end of town. The *hospitalera* was an elderly German. Jerry, the Irishman, was in the bed opposite. I thought of Michael and Jacques and decided they must have moved on, too. I had only walked fifteen kilometres that day.

We had a pleasant communal meal. The other pilgrims were Spanish. They were interested in me, the Australian, who had come so far. One had a distant relative in Australia. Another's son once visited. The evening was pleasant and quiet rather than boisterous with an opportunity to join a brief prayer service. The night was cool.

In the morning, the path continued its cold descent. The people thinned out and I became conscious of a real silence. I left the tarred road and followed a rough track across a series of hills. For so long I was always aware of traffic and/or people not far away, but for a welcome albeit brief time my world was silent and I experienced something of the profound solitude I felt on parts of the Camino in France.

My spirit responded and calmness descended.

I thought of nothing in particular and listened to my footfalls, as a kind of mantra which allowed me to engage with myself in a wonderful, self-sufficient and satisfying way. I was surrounded by the beauty of nature as I caught glimpses of the tarred road winding through the valleys below. I felt a sense of inner richness and of being refreshed and renewed.

But not for long! I descended to the tarred road and returned to the villages and eventually to Ponferrada. It takes its name from an iron bridge, rather normal these days but pretty impressive when built at the end of the 12th century.

A largely industrial town, it boasts an *albergue* at its

entrance. It was run by the parish and manned by volunteers, all of whom were older men. The *hospitaleros* were warm and friendly enough but the *albergue* was huge and the atmosphere impersonal.

I shared a room with Vincenzo – a Spaniard – and two Korean lads. The Koreans spoke a halting English but Vincenzo had none. I was intrigued how the Koreans came to know of the Camino. One of their older brothers, they told me, had completed it two years ago. My attendance at a Mass last year in Seoul suggested to me that the Korean Christian is very devout.

Jerry the Irishman was sitting in the courtyard. I joined him and we conversed for a good part of the afternoon. He was interested in the work I did with Lifeline, particularly in supporting the bereaved by suicide. He was grieving the death of his sister. He started at Astorga and was unlikely to reach Santiago this year because of limited time. He was walking during his holidays. This was the third year on the Camino. He started at Saint-Jean-Pied-de-Port and reached Astorga last year. It would take another year to reach Santiago. He worked for an organisation involved in training carers and often facilitated groups.

At dinner time the large kitchen and dining area was jam-packed with people trying to prepare and eat their meal. It reminded me of a scene from a comic film, everyone on top of each other and getting in one another's way. My Korean roommates recommended a restaurant with a pilgrims' menu and Jerry and I continued our chat.

They were playing Abba in the overcrowded kitchen in the morning. The *hospitaleros* had begun their cleaning tasks and I felt they were keen to be rid of their pilgrims. Ponferrada is an industrial town but it has a number of ancient buildings. I passed an impressively restored 13th century castle complete with drawbridge built by the Knights Templar.

My feet were feeling weary and I decided to take it easy, to limit myself to fifteen kilometres. I walked slowly and everyone passed me. As walkers passed, I would always turn to them with a greeting, usually a Spanish *Hola!* A larger number than usual were unresponsive, either grunting or ignoring me.

The number of walkers and cyclists had increased, particularly the groups. Like Jerry, many had started at Astorga. The walking was level through a number of attractive towns – Columbrianos, Fuentes Nuevas, and Camponaraya.

My destination was Cacabelos, formerly an important pilgrim town with five hospitals. I chose the municipal *albergue* at the far end of town. It was of quaint design, a series of two bed cabins around a wall surrounding a church.

My room companion was an older Spaniard. He spoke very good English and seemed an educated, self-composed professional. It would not have surprised me if he were a priest or even a bishop.

There was no kitchen or dining room so I walked back into the town for an evening meal and was sitting in a restaurant, ready to eat alone thinking that Jerry must have gone on when in he walked. He had had a bad night at Ponferrada with noisy snorers. He needed a decent sleep and went upmarket with a private room. We shared dinner and two bottles of wine. How quickly do you feel you get to know people! I had met Jerry only a few days previously but he seemed an old friend.

19. If the power of love was able to replace the love of power ...

Thisss morning I walked along a road through beautiful rolling country covered in vineyards to Villafranca de Bierzo.

While resting I noticed three older ladies also resting. Usually women walking together were chatty but these three were silent. When they left they walked in single file. They were among the few who walked more slowly than me and when I began walking I passed them. They did not respond to my usual greeting nor were they talking to each other. They walked solemnly, eyes on the ground before them. These same ladies passed me when I paused for a rest, and I caught up with them. I gave them little thought as I caught up with Jerry.

We walked along a river for a time, which would have been very beautiful but for the adjacent major freeway. We walked together through Pereje, a small village with overhanging balconies from one of which a small dog was barking furiously at every passer-by. There were plenty of noisy dogs along the Camino but this one was barking on high and was exceptional for its pint sized ferocity.

We continued on to Trabadelo, where we found the *albergue* and shared a room with two Finnish ladies and a German couple. The restaurant/bar was a good walk from the *albergue*. Here we shared a table with two other Finnish ladies, Maria (Mexican) and Marcel (Dutch). Maria and Marcel worked together in Germany. The Finns wanted to know about me. We had an interesting discussion on why people walked the Camino. Motivations ranged, they thought, from the deeply spiritual to the chance for a cheap walking holiday.

Jerry and I had a very pleasant stroll back to the *albergue*, one of the few times I had been walking at night in the dark. When I began walking in July, night did not descend until 10.00 pm but as the season progressed into autumn the sun set earlier. The night found us wrapped in awe at the sky above, full of stars – the milky way was used by pilgrims in centuries gone by to guide them as they walked ever due west. The term *Compostela* signifies the field of stars. I felt inspired, too and felt like grabbing my backpack from the *albergue* and continuing on but prudence and fatigue called me to my bed.

Jerry and I walked separately as we left the Camino about 7.00 am, both of us content with our own thoughts and reflections. The path became steep and as I moved towards Galicia, the fourth of the regions through which the Camino passes, I was reminded of the killer hills which had caused me so much pain last year. Every hill is a challenge.

The country was beautiful with many magnificent views. In France the hilly country afforded me silence and solitude but not here in Spain for the walkers and cyclists, wave after wave, continued their westward way. I passed the trio of ladies and they passed me. I continued to be intrigued. They walked in single file in the same order. They did not talk to each other and when they did it was in whispers. I tried to reach out to them each time I saw them.

'*Hola!*'

I hadn't yet worked out their language. Number three, the one who always walked behind struck me as timid and intimidated. She gave a faint awkward smile. Number two, the one

in the middle, ignored the world around her. Her gaze w
severe and her hair was dyed red. Number one, the one in fro₁
looked at me as if I were a troublesome child.

The climb continued steeply through the beautiful countryside. I met Jerry at La Laguna de Castilla, and rather than
continue to O'Cebreiro we stopped. The weather was hot and
Jerry found the heat trying. We enjoyed a beer in a shelter
opposite the bar which was also an *albergue*. The bar was playing what sounded like Irish music, which seemed incongruous
here in Spain but Jerry explained that Galicia has a strong
Celtic culture much the same as Ireland and Brittany. In the
past he had attended Celtic festivals both in Ireland and Brittany. We heard a few Irish tunes that afternoon.

In the *albergue* we found the three ladies ensconced. They
were relaxing and reading. They continued to be silent with the
occasional whisper to each other. I think it was in French. That
could explain their lack of response to my greeting in Spanish.
They continued to intrigue me. They were still uncommuni-
cative and I sensed a quiet anger in the redhead. I felt there
was tension between them. They did not appear to be a happy
trio. The other occupant of the dormitory was a Spanish lady.
The three of us had dinner together in the bar and when we
returned to the dormitory just on dark the three ladies were
already in bed. That was awkward as we tried to ready ourselves for bed and for the morning. One of the unwritten rules
of the Camino is to respect the other pilgrims. If someone is
trying to sleep, you are as quiet as possible and reduce any
light.

We fumbled around in the dark making full use of our
torches. Jerry, the Spanish lady and I rose about 6.30 am, but
the three ladies did not stir. In the dark and with the use of
our torches we fumbled around making more noise than if we

walking. He replied that he was thinking of leaving the organisation where he had worked for twenty years. He had been dissatisfied for a year or so, but found it difficult to move because of his fear of moving out of the comfort zone into the unknown. As if my question had helped him articulate his disquiet, he resolved that he would take action to find another job as soon as he returned to Ireland.

I said goodbye to Jerry. He was stopping at Sarria where he would take the bus to Santiago and thence to the airport. He said he would not visit the cathedral but save it for the time when he actually walked into Santiago as a pilgrim. He hoped that would be next year. I detected a touch of envy. I was continuing on. It was another sad farewell, which is part of the Camino journey. Just as you get to know someone, you have to go your separate ways.

I felt lonely again as I did when I left my other Camino friends. I remembered leaving Georg and Veronika, my young German friends, sitting at the bar at Calzadilla, where they decided not to go on further for the day because the seventeen kilometres walk from Carrion de los Condes had exhausted her. That was two weeks ago, but it seemed months. I wondered where they were now. Were they still behind me? Or had they slipped past me and gone ahead? Where was Michael, my one armed Danish friend? Had he already finished and was on his way home? I thought of our Camino romance, Jacob and Elena. Were they still together?

I turned my attention to the route. I reached Sarria after about 90 minutes and stopped to explore the hilly older part of the town with its churches, old houses and sites of former pilgrim hostels. I also came across some graffiti. The piece that stood out for me was written in English:

If the power of love was able to replace the love of power...

Galicia is noted for its strong winds and today the region lived up to its reputation. The wind carried the smell of rotting apples. The trees were full of fruit and the ground below was covered. At times you had to dodge them falling. The afternoon was cool with light rain. Just before I stopped for the night at Ferreiros, I passed the 100 kilometres marker stone. Many walkers had stopped here, too, for the stone was covered in messages and signatures. Astrid and Cyrano wanted the world to know they had passed by on 14.8.11 and placed their names in a large heart which covered the shell emblem. Many others recorded their names and date of arrival, but not as flamboyantly as Astrid and Cyrano.

After installing myself in the *albergue* and undertaking the usual chores, I conducted a recce of Ferreiros. The *hospitalera* told me there were two bars but the one further away had better meals. I passed the bar next to the *albergue* and walked about 300 metres to the other. It was also a restaurant and had an *albergue* attached.

As I walked back up the hill and neared the other bar, I was greeted very warmly. I responded warmly in return. I thought my friend was another pilgrim but I realised he was a local. He said he was Miguel and insisted on buying me a drink in the bar. As I was planning to have a beer, I followed him.

He was talking to me incessantly. I told him I didn't speak Spanish well, but that did not deter him. I reckoned Miguel had plenty to drink already. What made me uncomfortable was his excessive friendliness. My intention was to be polite and to hope I wasn't misjudging him but when he showed me with a sly smile some magazines he was carrying, my attitude changed. They contained photos of nude young men. I felt grubby, as if I was being propositioned. I've had to deal with unwelcome company in a bar before, and I was ready to say, 'I haven't a clue what you're saying, mate, but I don't want to hear any more so piss off', but he went outside.

I was happy to sit at a table with my beer. Two young Spanish pilgrims came in for a beer and sat opposite. When Miguel returned, he ignored me and turned his attention to the two young men. They responded to his friendliness and politely made a few comments in reply. Miguel continued to talk to them and appeared to be making a point. He used the Spanish word for 'pilgrim' a few times. I was intrigued to read their body language. Their attitude had changed from friendliness to indifference or hostility. The man behind the bar must have observed and called Miguel over. I asked the two in Spanish if they spoke English.

'A little,' one replied in English.

'Is that bloke talking bullshit?' I asked in English.

'Yes, of the worst kind,' he replied with a sigh.

I didn't bother to ask him to explain.

Meanwhile, the bar owner seemed to be telling Miguel it was time to go home. After much discussion, gestures and agitation Miguel left with a few bottles. I left shortly afterwards and paid for my beer. If I had to meet Miguel again I didn't want to be indebted to him and feel that I owed him a drink.

I walked down the hill to the other restaurant and had dinner with my two young Spanish friends. They had commenced at Sarria and had only a few days to get as far as they could. They were aiming to walk thirty plus kilometres each day, so I probably wouldn't see them again. They would get well ahead of me.

There was a door leading out to the back where I guessed the *albergue* lay. Who should walk through this door but Georg and Veronika. I called out to them and we greeted each other as long lost friends. We discussed some of our other friends, whether we had seen them or not. There was no kitchen in the albergue but they had come to ask the restaurant staff for a saucepan to cook their pasta. They were successful and back they went to the yard outside, where they had a gas burner.

I stayed with them while they cooked and shared a wine. As I left them I was tempted to ask Georg if he had found a double bed yet en route. As I walked back to the Camino under the field of stars, I had visions of Maris giving me a dressing-down for having such a cheeky thought.

Since leaving Pamplona thirty days previously, I had not given much thought to the future, just concentrated on the moment and living day by day. I had now walked nearly 700 kilometres since Saint-Jean-Pied-de-Port. I would be in Santiago by the end of the week.

What then?

I would have completed the physical journey but my inner spiritual journey would continue. Would I do things differently when I returned to Sydney? Before the end of the year I would see my seventy-ninth birthday. I was entering the final stages of my life, on the home run as it were. My body and mind were well past their peak. At the moment, my body was doing very well, thank you, just having brought me to this hill. I would like to think that when I got home, I would continue to enjoy a fulfilling life. I have never lost my sense of curiosity, a valued component of the spiritual life. I would continue to wonder and have my eyes opened.

I was forced to return to the present, to focussing on putting one foot in front of the other up the steep incline. *Just stay with the moment*, I reminded myself. *Get yourself up this hill, mate, intact and worry about those issues when the time comes.*

I hadn't given much thought to the past either and while I was having a drink in the bar next to the albergue at Gonzar I was in a reflective mood and read back over my journal. I read about the many people I had met and wondered where they were now. In addition to the people my notes reminded me of special moments, of the beauty of nature which I had witnessed, of sunflowers, sun rises and fields of stars, where I felt the presence of a creative force so vast that I felt insignificant. I had discovered that the Camino is about peaks and valleys, never a level playing field. I've learned to travel through both just as I have learned to travel through the peaks and valleys of life. I'd like to think my life journey has given me maturity, understanding and wisdom.

Back in the present, sipping my beer and reading, I heard the sound of cows bellowing. The bar and *albergue* were close to cow sheds. In fact, Galicia was cow country and an additional hazard of the Camino was avoiding the cow shit.

I didn't get to know any of the other pilgrims and I was happy to dine on my own in my solitude and to retire to bed early. I was alone without being lonely. The *albergue* was noisy with the thunder of trucks reverberating during the night.

20. Like a crowd coming out of a football match

I met Georg and Veronika at one of the bars next morning. Georg was ever the comedian, full of jokes and life. I walked with them to Palas de Rei, but it was too early to stop so I said goodbye and pushed on to a tiny village by name San Xulian where I found a bar/restaurant and *albergue* opposite.

I shared a room with two others. Barry was Canadian and ex-navy. Mario, despite his Italian name, was a young German cyclist and student. Barry had spent all his working life in the Navy. He had never married; his life was the Canadian Navy. He had enjoyed walking some of the trails in the Canadian wilderness, hence his interest in the Camino; but he found looking after himself and organising his itinerary a challenge because he had been used to receiving movement orders which told him where and when to be somewhere. Mario was the first cyclist with whom I had a good conversation. He showed me his bicycle and his various gadgets. He explained that whereas walkers could set out before dawn, cyclists had to wait for the light because it was too dangerous to cycle in the dark.

Everyone dined together in the bar opposite. I shared a table with a group of Germans who were walking for ten days. They were intrigued at my age and nationality. Why was I on the Camino? Why had I come all this way? How often was I asked that question?

Barry had departed by the time I woke. I left shortly after 7.00 am, leaving Mario in bed. One of the first walkers I saw was a young dark-skinned lady, very slim and elegant. She told me unannounced that she was going to have a great day today. I wondered about her comment, as if she was psyching herself for a better day than she had previously.

I paused to eat my breakfast and sat on a stone wall. Mario passed on his bicycle and gave a cheery wave. I was surprised at the crowd of walkers who passed me. I guessed many had started at Sarria. They came in waves, walking in twos and threes, sometimes a larger group, making plenty of noise with their chatter and the clatter of their sticks on the asphalt. No chance of silence or solitude here! Everyone seemed to be in a hurry as if they were in a race to outdo each other or keen to get to the next *albergue* before all the beds were taken. Some had inadequate footwear. I wondered how many would arrive exhausted and suffering the pain of blistered feet.

One of the rules for gaining the *Compostela* certificate at Santiago was that you had to show evidence of having walked at least 100 kilometres. I was not sure of my attitude towards these latecomers. I would show the authorities my *credencial* filled with stamps all the way from Le Puy, over 1500 kilometres; others would show evidence of only 100 kilometres. We would get the same certificate.

I was reminded of the parable of the vineyard labourers told in Matthew's gospel which I'd heard many times. A landowner went out at daybreak to hire workers for his vineyard. He agreed to pay them one denarius. He kept coming out during the day to hire more workers right up to the eleventh hour. Everyone received a denarius. Those who had worked through the heat of the day grumbled for receiving the same as the eleventh hour types. Even as a child, I always thought the day-long labourers had been hard done by and was sympathetic to their claim. As a hardcore pilgrim I was intolerant of the Johnny-come-latelies and had to remind myself to be charitable. Each walks according to his or her own resources and timeframe. Many had the constraints of work and family. The important thing is that all had attempted the Camino and some had more time.

At Melide I came across Peter, the Irishman, sitting in a bar and I joined him for a coffee. I made a comment about the large number of walkers. He had noticed the same. It reminded him of the crowd coming out of a football game. I planned to stop at Ribadiso because someone had mentioned it had a very nice *albergue* but with the crowds of walkers passing me I was anxious whether there would be room. I pushed myself to walk faster. At one stage a local came out of his house as I passed and told me I was on the wrong road. I was grateful but I was frantic because I had lost time in retracing my steps. Anxiety got the better of me and I was infected with the virus of competition.

There was no need to worry. There was plenty of room. I even found a bottom bunk. Most of the pilgrims were probably aiming for Arzua, just a few kilometres further on. The *albergue* lived up to expectations. It had the feeling of an ancient pilgrim hospice that had been restored. It was located just by a river and I had a vision of the ancient pilgrims stripping off and splashing around in the cooling waters.

The opportunities to wash were infrequent in those days. Being a hot day, the modern pilgrims were splashing and sunbathing in their shorts and bikinis. Among the sunbathers was the dark-skinned lady who told me she was going to have a great day. She looked as if she was, for she had attracted the attention of the young men. I envied them. She was beautiful in her bikini.

I had my turn to talk to her because she occupied the top

bunk. She was French from Paris, just walking for a few days. I'd be lying if I said I didn't have some lustful images, the thought of her lovely young body just above me. I was no better than the young blokes.

The bar/restaurant next door was very busy. I introduced Barry to Peter, and together we dined with a German named Josef. Josef was very quiet.

People were getting up early about 5.30 am and in their efforts to be quiet in the dark, they made a lot of noise. I rose early too and in no time I was walking through Arzua only three kilometres on. The large number of walkers already on the road reminded me of Peter's comment 'like a crowd coming out of a football match.'

The hardcore pilgrims who had been walking hundreds of kilometres regarded these newcomers as tourists. I had to remind myself that everyone has a different journey, short or long. I walked for a while with an Australian. Wendy was from Dapto south of Sydney. We were nostalgic at the sight of blue gums standing straight and tall in plantations. The sight and smell of eucalyptus reminded me so much of the Australian bush that I half expected a wallaby or two to come bounding past. These blue gum forests were to extend to and past Santiago and from time to time I came across loggers harvesting the mature trees for their timber.

At Arca de Pino I had my first knockback! The first *albergue* was full. I felt a faint sour panic which seemed to cling to a place until I'd found myself a bed. I got one at the large communal just up the road. An impatient *hospitalera* tapped the table with her pencil, bored witless as I struggled to find my passport and *credencial*.

I shared a cubicle with two dentists from Ireland. One was red-haired, freckled and Irish. The other was Italian and was leaving Dublin to work in London. They had taken four days off to walk and celebrate the new job. I had dinner with these two when I learned about the practice of dentistry in Ireland, which I added to what Peter had told me about the practice of football.

As I woke, I remembered that this day I should reach Santiago, only twenty kilometres away. I had walked 750 kilometres, carried my pack all the way and never succumbed to the temptation of catching the bus or having my baggage sent on. In one way I was anxious to reach the destination, Santiago, but in other ways I was in no hurry. Santiago would not be the end of my Camino for I had the time to continue walking to Finisterre.

After clearing the town I walked through extensive eucalyptus forests accompanied by crowds of other walkers passing me in great numbers. I felt that if someone panicked and broke into a run, everyone would follow, such was the feeling of competition in the air, something I had not experienced up to this time.

The ambiance of the Camino had changed.

I walked for a time with Josef. He told he was from a small village in Germany and did not like towns. He found the Camino too crowded. I had to agree with him and told him it was not like this further back. There one had time for silence and solitude.

I walked with Jill from London. She had walked the Camino previously and told me that this was the low season and that the numbers had fallen compared with the high season of July/August. I was amazed. If this was the low season, the high season's numbers must be staggering. I had visions of the Camino's infrastructure collapsing under the flood of pilgrims pushing each other out of the way in the race for a bed.

I had considered stopping the night at San Marcos and walk the extra five kilometres in the morning but I arrived early. What a crowd around the monument! A large modern sculpture marks the spot from where the pilgrims could see the cathedral at Santiago for the first time after their long journey and so it was named Mount Joy (*Monte del Gozo*). My guidebook told me that it was once a quiet hill but the area was levelled to make way for the vast crowd that attended the Mass for the Pope's visit in 1989. The numbers today were nowhere near as vast but there were plenty of pilgrims milling around, eating their lunch or buying drinks and ice creams from the stalls.

Beyond the sculpture I passed a large complex, a cross between army barracks and a scout camp, with accommodation for 3000 people.

I continued on.

Like the entry to many cities, the outskirts of Santiago are dreary and uninviting and it's not until you reach the old city that you see something of the destination that pilgrims have sought down the centuries. Most pilgrims seem to hurry to the cathedral after arriving in Santiago but I decided to seek accommodation and visit the cathedral early the next day before the crowds arrived.

There were plenty of options for a bed but I chose the *Seminario Menor* and booked myself in for two nights. The *albergue* was enormous with imposing columns and steps leading up to the entrance – in its day no doubt a grand building housing students for the priesthood. The good news was that they had private rooms so for five euros extra I had the luxury, after forty nights of sharing with up to thirty people, of sleeping on my own.

After the usual chores, I walked into the old city and found a bar and sat in the window with a beer. The window looked out on a road crossing at the Porto do Camino, which led up to the cathedral so there was plenty of traffic. Many were wearing their backpacks and seemed in a hurry to reach their destination. Others appeared to have discarded their packs, cleaned themselves up and were now, like me, exploring the town.

I enjoyed watching the people gathering at the lights, waiting, a few dashing across through light traffic, the rest surging across with the green light. I saw Barry crossing the road towards me. Barry always had a lost expression as if he still hadn't quite adjusted to his having to sort out everything for himself now he was out of the Canadian Navy, which did all his thinking for him. He seemed more confused than usual. I dashed out and greeted him and invited him to join me at the window. Yes, he was confused. He had arrived the day before and had spent the day exploring. He had seen all manner of things but he couldn't remember where.

A few minutes later, I was thrilled to see another familiar face – Michael, my one-armed mate from Denmark. Again, I dashed out and we embraced each other on the footpath as if we were old friends who'd been separated for years rather for days. I was thrilled because I thought I would never see him again. I thought that he had already returned home. No, he said, he was leaving the next day. He had been in Santiago, taken the bus to Finisterre, and now his Camino was coming to its conclusion. He joined us in the bar at the window, and the three of us drank, talked and watched the people crossing the road.

We moved about three doors to a restaurant and over dinner and several bottles of Spanish wine shared our experiences. As usual Michael was a fund of Camino gossip. He told us of meeting a young Norwegian couple running the Camino for their honeymoon. I had seen this couple a few days earlier jumping from rock to rock down a stony path. They scared me for their recklessness and I hoped neither would fall.

Michael also mentioned sharing a meal with a young Austrian who had walked out of his marriage literally straight on to the Camino. As I listened to his stories, it occurred to me that I knew little about Michael. He was garrulous enough but he had built a hedge of words about him that hid his secrets from the world.

Both Michael and Barry were staying at the *Seminario Menor* so we ambled slowly back in time for the curfew. Michael's room was two down from mine, so in the passageway, we embraced, let go of each other and said goodbye.

21. I've been to the end of the Earth and back

With no early risers rustling in the dark, I slept late. This was my first rest day in thirty-five days. I was planning to take it easy, just exploring. A fog had descended on the town and in the mist I walked back past my bar, over the crossing at Porto do Camino, up the hill and down to the cathedral. This building was my goal, the destination of all the pilgrims following the Way of St James. Here lay the tomb of Saint James the Apostle.

What a spectacle!

The cathedral is part Romanesque, part Baroque, with a magnificent Portico de la Gloria and façade giving onto the Plaza del Obradoiro.

Before entering I walked across the Plaza and to the rear of the cathedral to collect my *Compostela*, a certificate written in Latin certifying I had walked the Camino. To obtain it the pilgrim had to produce the *credencial* stamped at the various locations along the way. By now I had used three to cover my 1500 kilometres, stamped at the *gîtes*, *albergues*, bars, churches, and any other establishment which had a pilgrims' stamp. I found the Pilgrims' Office.

If I were a romantic and expected to be handed my *Compostela* with ceremony, I would have been disappointed. I joined the queue which wound its way through a courtyard, up a flight of stairs and into an office where bureaucracy and efficiency ruled the day. They were organised for crowds. A sign above the door told the waiting pilgrim which counter was vacant. I was reminded of the many times I've queued in the bank for the next teller.

The lady was efficiency personified. She noted my nationality then inspected my *credencial*. She dropped her formality for a moment to congratulate me in English for my 1500 kilometres and entered my details into her computer. She had to consult a colleague for the Latin equivalent of Noel. The computer printed my *Compostela* with my name in copperplate writing: *Nicolaum Josephum Braun* dated *17 Septembris 2011*.

Up to that time I had dealt with arriving at the cathedral and joining the queue in a matter of fact way, but as I looked at my certificate on the way out past the pilgrims who had joined the line after me, emotion swelled and tears flowed. I couldn't believe it. I had completed the project. I began walking last year and I had been planning for years. The Camino had occupied my mind for so long. Like the forces of gravity it had drawn me over mountains, across plains, in heat and rain, through dust and mud. And now I'd made it. I had achieved my goal. I needed time on my own. A little solitude was essential to explore my feelings and regain some balance. I entered the cathedral and found a seat in the second row, prepared to wait a good hour for the pilgrims' Mass at midday.

I didn't take much notice of the incredibly ornate altar and sanctuary with its gold leaf and semi naked angels. I didn't join the queue waiting to enter the crypt to view Saint James' tomb. I sat in a pew and wept. Out of the blue I felt the grief of losing Maris as intensely as when she first died. I was having a major meltdown. I was overwhelmed by a hollowness, as if my innards were being scooped out. I bowed my head and the tears rolled down my cheeks. Around me the cathedral was filling with a mass of people.

In the hour I waited a dozen or more tour groups arrived

each with their flag-waving leader trying to explain in a variety of languages the features of the cathedral all the time a priest on his microphone calling for silence. Santiago is a tourist mecca, on the itinerary of every tour company. Dozens of coaches arrive daily and this Saturday was no exception. In addition, there were organised groups of pilgrims, some of them singing, wearing the same uniform, one of their number carrying a banner. Many pilgrims were wearing their backpacks as if they had rushed to get to the cathedral in time for the Mass. The building was full. Some had walked hundreds of kilometres, some the last hundred, others were walking for the weekend and the tourists had arrived by coach.

The priest on the microphone managed to quieten the chaos. The noisy crowd settled down for Mass. In the second row I had a good view but around me were tourists well-dressed with their designer handbags taking up the seats while tired pilgrims had to stand. A group of these tourists arrived late and tried to stand in the space between the altar rails and the pews but an attendant chased them away. I chastised myself for my uncharitable thoughts about tourists, spectators rather than participants.

About twelve priests arrived to celebrate the pilgrim Mass in much the same way as it was celebrated for the pilgrims of a thousand years ago. Instead of Latin this Mass was in Spanish but I understood the pilgrims' welcome and the list of countries from which the pilgrims had arrived. I didn't hear Australia mentioned so I guessed they were working with yesterday's figures. Australia would get a mention tomorrow.

My emotions were raw from my grief. They touched a deep place. I felt the presence of millions of pilgrims who had pressed into this building down the centuries. After battling with the elements, fatigue, pain and their own demons, they had arrived in this sacred place, overwhelmed by their feelings and the joy of arriving.

After Mass I was in a mess. I drifted around the building, feeling disoriented, vulnerable and uncertain. I needed to talk to someone. Around the walls were confessionals and some were operating, a priest inside and a penitent kneeling at his window.

One had a notice announcing that confession was heard in Spanish, French and English. I joined his queue.

I confessed to being intolerant and mentioned that I had had this strong emotional reaction. The kindly priest replied that I was not alone. Many people have an intense experience on arriving in Santiago, he explained. The opportunity to talk had its therapeutic effect.

With a sigh of relief I regained my equilibrium, sat in front of the main altar, compelling in all its decoration. I felt subdued as if something deep inside me had been touched. I was in solitary mood and content to talk to no one. After the catharsis of the Pilgrim Mass I spent the remainder of my rest day quietly and ate a pizza for dinner.

Most of the people I had spoken to along the way were only going as far as Santiago. I wasn't ready to stop. I had a week to spare as my flight to Paris was booked for the following Sunday. The week would allow me to wind down before making the transfer back to 'normal' life.

I left the *Seminario Menor* about 7.30 am and walked through a silent Santiago. Outside the town precincts I climbed a hill and looked back to see the cathedral silhouetted against the rising sun, the rest of the town in shadow. The cathedral dominates Santiago. The way led me through shimmering blue gum forests. I was surprised at the extensive plantings. The undergrowth of bracken and the Spanish ground strewn with fallen strips of bark added to the appearance of an Australian bush landscape. I was nostalgic to be home.

What a contrast! After the last 100 kilometres of battling with crowds of walkers, I had the track to myself. I didn't have to worry about being trampled down by a herd of Spanish talking at the top of their voices to no one else but themselves, or being knocked aside in the rush to get the last bed in the *albergue*. An exaggeration but that was the drift of my thinking.

I met a group of Norwegians. Everyone commented on the large number of walkers in the last 100 kilometres and talked about the relief of getting out of Santiago.

The Camino was peaceful with the reduced numbers. I had a sense of solitude and silence which I did not often experience in Spain. Now in my solitude I felt the stirrings of my inner life. I regained the feeling of being in touch with Creation even though I was walking through an artificial forest, one that had been planted with a foreign tree.

Still, one could argue that the Creator was working through the human hands that planted and cared for these trees. I was in a sacred place. One day they would cut down the trees, but until they were harvested, they offered grace and beauty. I would like to think that the area offered to pilgrims a place of calm and peace after the hurly burly of Santiago. I was feeling well. The rest day had done me good. It was a beautiful sunny day with a cooling breeze and even the killer hills were tolerable.

My mood was nostalgic. None of my friends of the Camino had gone past Santiago so I did not expect to see any familiar faces. I crossed the barrier from solitude into loneliness. Added to my loneliness of sorts the Australian bush around me rendered me homesick and I thought about the many times I had been bushwalking. I shed an occasional tear, I'm afraid to say. Perhaps this was to be expected because I was in the winding down phase of my Camino. I had completed the task.

I came across a group of Germans. They turned out to be an organised group with a tour leader. Teresa was Spanish, spoke German and had a smattering of English. She was intrigued about my age and nationality. She wanted a photo of her with me. She was tiny and didn't come up to my armpits but she was a lively lady with a contagious enthusiasm – the right temperament for organising a group of dour middle-aged Germans.

I met the Norwegians again. They, too, were intrigued at my nationality and age and asked to take my photo. In contrast to tiny Angela their tour leader was a huge man. Finn was a Lutheran minister and regularly took groups of pilgrims. Both groups had started at Santiago and were walking to Finisterre.

The municipal *albergue* at Vilaserio was located in the old school. It had no beds, just mattresses on the floor, so I opted for the *Albergue touristico O Ruerio*, run by the *Bar A Nosa Casa*. I enjoyed a relaxing afternoon gazing at the tall blue gums towering over the tiny village.

The *albergue's* computer was working and Bigpond was operating so I was able to read the family's emails. Their moral support had me weepy again. I thanked God for my family and the encouragement they gave me, their mad tearful parent who, instead of sitting quietly at home in a rocking chair like other sensible seventy-eight-year-olds, careens around the world.

Next morning was misty but eventually became a warm sunny day. I walked through more blue gum forests but eventually they thinned out and disappeared. I said goodbye to my trees as if I was taking leave of old friends. I know that those trees weren't planted for me but they had been my companions since entering Galicia.

As my gum trees passed behind my thoughts turned to Maris. I left my body walking along the track while my mind moved to another time and place, to the day she died and all its detail. I thought of her every day on the Camino and usually admonished myself not to dwell too long on her death but to think of her life.

This time I stayed in the dark places longer. I felt the same feelings, first of apprehension and dread as I was desperately waiting for her to complete an errand from which she never returned. Then the realisation that something dreadful had happened when the police arrived. And then the grief when the doctor at the Royal North Shore Hospital told me her body was in the next room.

My life was changed forever on that warm, humid Saturday afternoon. What might have been if she was still with me? I would not be walking the Camino. I would not have that hollow feeling which keeps me restless and searching. I would be home in Sydney with her, content to be with her and to care for her.

I was pleased when the arrival of Teresa and her Germans bought me back to the present. She was keen for another round of photographs and was enthusiastically organising me and her group.

They were heading for Olveiroa and so was I, but they stayed at the *pension* while I stayed at the municipal *albergue*, a series of stone buildings built in the traditional style. I was among the first to arrive and selected my room of three beds.

At first I shared with a wiry shrivelled Frenchman, the skinniest pilgrim to date. I went out to explore the village and when I returned I found two young Portuguese. The girl was on the last bed and the boy was on a mattress on the floor. The two continued to chatter while the Frenchman and I tried to rest, one of the few occasions when I witnessed a lack of respect for fellow pilgrims. Their friends were in other parts of the *albergue* and continued to visit.

The Portuguese boy was one of the few fellow pilgrims I disliked. He annoyed me with his chatter but, as they were not going to let me rest, I talked to him and the girl as they both had some English. They had started the day before and were walking for four days. I felt they were quite unprepared. The boy, whose name was Diego, told me they never walked. His feet were evidence; they were in a bad way. He had several blisters and he was suffering. He let everyone know.

I said to him, 'You don't believe in suffering in silence.'

He quietened down but his body language communicated his continued pain. I wondered how he would survive the next two days.

The bar/restaurant was next door and I joined a mixed group. One German told me he had walked the Camino eight times. His first effort was in 1995. I asked about the differences since then. He mentioned the crowds of today. When he first stayed at Olveiroa, the facilities were primitive. His comment that the *albergue* had been constructed since then impressed me as the buildings could have been hundreds of years old, albeit restored.

The Portuguese woke very early and, as they had no torches, stumbled around in the dark trying to find and pack their things. They woke both me and the skinny Frenchman, so I got up and turned on the light. That made things easier for everyone. Diego was not as brash or talkative as the previous evening but he was still suffering, in silence this time, but his body language and grim expression told the world he was the martyr set for a bad day. I usually felt sorry for my fellow pilgrims in pain but, God forgive me, not this morning.

The day was fine but very windy. Galicia was living up to its reputation of being the windiest part of Spain. It also had a reputation for being the wettest, but so far no rain had fallen on my parade. I kept on meeting Teresa and her Germans and eventually I met them again at the end of the plateau to witness a view of the track falling down to the beach and the sea. There was the Atlantic Ocean stretched out before me. I had walked all this way from the Pyrenees. I really was near my objective.

My last day of walking was brief. The track followed the coastline around a bay and visited a number of beaches which would have been a mecca for holiday makers. By late September the season was well past so the bars, resorts and camping sites were closed for winter.

The day was warm and sunny and the sky was cloudless and blue. As the town of Finisterre came in sight I walked along the beach. In the season I imagine this beautiful beach would have been crowded but now only a handful was strolling. I picked up a shell, which has become one of the precious souvenirs of my Camino. It's my link with the past. I had joined those medieval pilgrims who had taken home a shell from the Galician beaches.

I had to wait in the queue outside the municipal *albergue* until it opened at 1.00 pm. Once I had my bed I dumped my pack and walked the three kilometres to the lighthouse. I passed the last marker with its line of zeros. I had reached my destination. I had arrived at the end of the Earth.

I met Teresa and her Germans. She insisted on photos around the marker. Beyond the lighthouse I scrambled down the rocks almost to the water's edge and threw the last remaining rock that I had brought from home into the water. That was my symbolic act of completion. I had left something of myself behind.

I looked around me. A few like me had ventured down the rocks and had perched themselves on vantage points but the majority had stayed on top by the lighthouse. I sat for quite a while perched on a ledge over the ocean where someone before me had left the remnants of a small shrine in an alcove, a tiny cross and a burnt out candle.

I stared out across the vast water. I listened to the waves splashing on the rocks. The sea was gentle but I imagined its fury in a storm. I wondered how many pilgrims over the ages had scrambled down these rocks and stared into the distance. I was in touch with eternity, with countless numbers who had reached the end of the Earth.

I offered a prayer of thanks. I thanked God every morning for having the physical health and stamina to undertake the Camino but this prayer was special. I had achieved my objective.

I felt a tear and wished Maris was with me, both our hearts full of gratitude and staring across the oceans to America.

I lost track of time but eventually I climbed back, being extra careful. I did not want to slip and break a limb at this last moment, but as I reached the top I realised I had over two years walked 1500 kilometres in solitary endurance over innumerable hills, along the roughest of tracks and dangerous roads heavy with traffic, mostly under clear skies but sometimes in heavy rain. I had come out unscratched. I felt sad but I was happy to leave the killer hills behind.

Teresa invited me to coffee with her group and eventually I said goodbye to this group of middle-aged affluent Germans. Another parting. Back in the town I found an internet café and sent an email to the family saying I was at Finisterre, ninety kilometres beyond Santiago, right on the Atlantic, thought by the ancients to be the most western part of Europe. I'd been to the end of the world and back.

The following morning I awoke to a thick fog. I was lucky I had done my sightseeing on such a clear day. I had a sense of contentment as I took the bus ride back to Santiago.

I booked myself into the *Seminario Menor*, again in a private room. As I had been carrying only one change in my backpack I decided I needed some extra clothes so I went shopping.

The fog stayed around all day and only thinned out as evening approached. I had a long siesta in the afternoon and didn't do much else except take up a position in the window of my favourite bar and watched the people crossing the road at Porto do Camino, hoping to see a familiar face.

There were many pilgrims hurrying across to the cathedral but none I knew. The people I'd met would have left and a new wave had replaced them. It reminded me of the water in a river. As soon as one lot passes another replaces them

I walked to the cathedral early in order to beat the weekend crowds. In contrast to last week when the queue to go down into the crypt extended around the building, I walked straight down the steps to inspect the tomb of Saint James. I attended the 9.00 am Mass and saw the famous *botafumeiro* in action.

It's probably the biggest incense burner in the world. It's made of silver and so heavy that it took a team of eight men to set it in motion, swinging at ceiling height from one end of the transept to the other, all the while spewing out the incense smoke the function of which in medieval days was to cover the smell of the unwashed pilgrims.

I visited a few of the souvenir shops but returned to the cathedral for the midday Mass. I was surprised at the smaller crowd. In contrast to the previous Saturday there were fewer tour groups and tourists and everyone had a seat.

I felt myself calm and relaxed until I saw a young man taking a photograph of his partner in front of the altar. A simple ordinary act I saw all the time, but this time it reminded me I was without partner, and I felt the loss. It just takes something simple and unexpected.

In the afternoon I managed a haircut and did the round of souvenir shops in earnest and bought a T shirt, cap and fridge magnet for myself as well as a few items for the family. The extra weight in my backpack did not matter now.

I found a market stall on the way back to the *Albergue*, which stocked some English classics. For three euros I bought a copy of Stephen Crane's *The Red Badge of Courage* to read on the plane the following day.

22. If you wish to be sure of the road you're travelling, close your eyes and walk in the dark

A rriving at Santiago was not the end of my pilgrimage. Pilgrimages are circular. You come but you don't stay. You travel along a route, arrive at your goal but the journey continues in the days and months and years that follow your return to where you come from. I was on my way home but my pilgrimage continued in that I had a further destination. My French book *Guide Spirituel du Pèlerin* recommended that, following the Camino, the pilgrim should undertake a monastic retreat and included a list of French monasteries. I visited Chartres cathedral in 2010. I found walking the labyrinth an uplifting experience and an opportunity for a prayer of movement. I wanted to do the same in 2011, a fitting finale to walking the Camino.

In addition to reading *The Red Badge of Courage*, the day and a half of travel from Santiago to Chartres gave me time to nourish my inner spiritual life. The Camino had stimulated my imagination. I had a glimpse the possibilities of eternal truths in my encounter with the sunflowers and the 'Breath of God' one morning at dawn.

I was inspired at the courage of many people who had left the comfort of their homes to undertake such an arduous journey and despite their suffering continued to persist. They were searching and, like me, had some difficulty in articulating the reasons for undertaking this arduous endeavour.

Surfing the internet I discovered that the Faith Hope and Love Global Ministries would be running a contemplative pilgrimage, a spiritual retreat at Chartres cathedral in the same week that I had scheduled my visit. I was familiar with the Ministry because I had read a book – *Praying the Labyrinth* – written by one of the retreat leaders, Jill Geoffrion, which I bought at Grace Cathedral in San Francisco when I walked the labyrinth there in 2006.

I had exchanged emails with Jill. She and her husband Tim would be the retreat leaders. Why not join them? I was open to what the retreat had to offer. I liked the warmth that radiated from Jill's emails and her promotional blurb – I also liked the enigmatic quotation from St John of the Cross at the end of her emails: *If you wish to be sure of the road you are travelling close your eyes and walk in the dark.*

My last experience of retreats was at school, which were appropriate at that stage of my life, but now, many years later, I had a completely different perspective and a different set of questions. Spirituality changes over time. The development of spirituality is a lifelong journey. I was apprehensive because I wasn't sure what to expect. Both Jill and Tim were American pastors. Fixed in my mind was a stereotype of yanks going overboard.

Would I find myself under siege weathering the evangelistic storm that I'd seen on early morning religious TV programmes? I was expecting to be challenged. I was stepping out of a comfort zone, but that has seldom deterred me from leaping into the unknown. Faith and spirituality are about moving out of your comfort zone, trusting in the lead given and knocking down the barricades to let the unknown in. Furthermore, both Jill and Tim had read my book *No Way to Behave at a Funeral* and I was encouraged by the insight of their comments.

What about *The Red Badge of Courage*? I chose this book because I'd read it years before and knew it to be an exciting account of the American Civil War to pass the time travelling. It's a classic of American literature and regarded as one of the best accounts of war from an ordinary soldier's perspective.

I did not expect it to have much relevance to my week at Chartres. I chose it as a secular contrast but I found a profoundly moving account of one young man's battle with himself to overcome uncertainty and doubt. He was facing enormous challenges on a spiritual journey of self-discovery. I identified with this young soldier.

So I came to Chartres with a very open mind, ready to listen and to learn. I was familiar with the beauty of the cathedral and the value of the labyrinth. The labyrinth was installed on the floor of the nave between 1194 and 1220. Its single path design represents the journey of the spirit. It's a path of prayer and reflection, walked for spiritual insight and healing. A labyrinth differs from a maze in that a maze is designed to lose your way whereas the labyrinth leads you on a path to a destination. It's a metaphor for our own spiritual journey in much the same way as the Camino is a metaphor.

When I first walked the labyrinth in 2006 I likened the pathway to my life up to the moment, the various turns being the important events in my life, the most significant being the presence of Maris – our life together and her death. The pathway is clearly defined. I could see where I'd been. The sense of being open to what lay ahead came as I left the confines of the labyrinth. I was moving into the future, into the unknown. When I visited in 2010, a question arose as I walked around the path. What is the next step for me? It was a question that couldn't be answered immediately. It was as if I had to be patient, to live with the question and, one of these days, live into the answer. Would I find an answer on this third visit?

Jill and Tim warmly welcomed their pilgrims. In no way did I feel intimidated but an equal among pilgrims on the journey. Jill was enthusiastic and devotional. She loved the cathedral and the labyrinth. Her enthusiasm was infectious. Tim had an engaging style. He was a good teacher and guided his pilgrims through thought-provoking questions, discussions and personal reflection. The two enjoyed their complementary skills.

I was surprised at the small number of pilgrims. Besides me, there were five others, all Americans. Cheryl was from New York, Beth, Jane and Maureen from Minneapolis, and MJ. I'm not sure where she lived.

I got to know these people in our discussions and our shared prayers and meals. We spent time in the cathedral, just a few minutes from the retreat centre. Although I have visited many cathedrals in Europe, the Chartres Cathedral is the one that I have had the privilege to study closely. The building is breathtaking. If you visit as a tourist you will find an outstanding model of aesthetic achievement but, if you visit as a pilgrim, you will enter a wonderful instrument of religious action, of a faith expressed in stone that generates its own energy. If you give yourself the time to appreciate the beauty, to absorb its harmony, and not rush on to the next tourist thing, it's difficult not to be inspired.

I found myself so often just wandering around, looking about me, at the soaring roof, at the magnificent stained glass windows, at the carvings and sculptures, all the time giving thanks for the opportunity to linger in such a place. I felt an affinity with the millions of visitors over the centuries, of the multitude of pilgrims whose feet had worn smooth the stone of the labyrinth, of the countless everyday folk whose efforts built the cathedral stone by stone and have kept it going since. What extraordinary vision had the original designers! How did they manage to get things just right?

One afternoon, we left Chartres and on a beautifully sunny day visited the original quarry from which the stone came. The quarry had been a working enterprise until only recently. The people of the village came out to meet us. We were shown the actual places from which the stone had been extracted. Those stones were carted back the ten kilometres to the cathedral site. The trip became a pilgrimage in itself with everyone – even royalty – participating.

We walked back to Chartres following their route. We didn't have to carry large stones, just tiny pieces of rocks as souvenirs. It would have been difficult to get lost because we walked across a plain with the cathedral on the horizon, its towers soaring up to the cloudless sky. Even in these modern times the cathedral is a dominant landmark in the countryside.

Like everyone else, we were able to walk the labyrinth on Friday when the chairs were cleared away. However, we were allowed into the cathedral after closing time on Thursday evening. We helped moved the chairs to one side and had the labyrinth to ourselves. Then with all the time in the world we walked the labyrinth.

On my last visits the thinking side of me was dominant, thinking about my past and my future, where I was going in my life without Maris, etc. without too much reference to the present moment. This time was different. I put my thinking aside and put on my feeling cap. I just walked and was intent on the experience of being there. I realised on the Camino that the action of walking was a prayer in itself. One doesn't pray just with words. You can pray with body movement and by just being present. The labyrinth acted as a metaphor bridging spirit and body, integrating the whole of my being, my masculine and feminine sides, the rational with the emotional, my physical and spiritual journeys.

I had brought from Australia the small wooden cross made from pieces of driftwood which I found on an Oregon beach. I had carried it in my backpack but now I held it in my hands.

My cross is sacred to me. It's a link with eternity. Who knows? The tree from which came the wood of my cross could have been growing at the time the labyrinth was built. I felt myself floating timelessly. Sometimes I felt a presence, just like on the Camino. Sometimes Maris was walking with me, sometimes Jesus. I used to tell the others that I regarded Jesus, not as the distant king of heaven, but as my mate and he spoke with an Aussie accent. I'd like to think that either Maris or Jesus was telling me not to be too worried about where I was going. Just be content to be. I already knew this because about a month before I left Australia, I came across a series of quotations from Thomas Merton, one of which was:

You do not need to know precisely what is happening, or exactly where it is all going. What you need is to recognise the possibilities and challenges offered by the present moment, and to embrace them with courage, faith and hope.

What has happened to me at Chartres? What did it add to my Camino experience? I think my eyes have been opened wider to the many ways in which God is present in our lives and to the many ways in which we can pray. My time with Tim and Jill was only a start. Much was enlivened in the time but I could see that my first task was not to let the week slip into the mists of memory. I had to continue to nurture all the learning and insights. I had a job to do, as if the week had been a briefing on the work ahead. I could not go home and be complacent, or slip back into the comfortable old ways of thinking. I had to go home with a sense of dissatisfaction. I needed to do something different with my spiritual life.

I needed to do a critical review. Before I began the Camino I raised the question *Who am I?* and *What do I want to become?* I also reflected on my allegiance to the Catholic Church.

A central principle of its social justice teaching is respect for the individual and the common good. Such teaching can be very demanding in what it expects from me. In becoming who I want to be most deeply and truly I should move away from considering myself in individual private terms and reflect on my position in the world around me – as a member of my family, my neighbourhood, my country, my church, my culture and my planet – if I want to grow spiritually. I'll have to pose a series of questions. What is hard about growing spiritually? What'll get in the way and undermine my spiritual enthusiasm and vitality? What'll keep me from pursuing my vision? What help will I need to stay on the path?

I'll need to face reality. God gave me a spirit which can get lofty at times but He gave me a body as well, grounded with its needs and desires. I can be a selfish bugger. I need to face the truth about myself, discard the delusions, stop kidding myself and come to grips with what I don't want to see. I need to seek inner change. This would require a prayer or two to help me to see what I need to see, to give me the guts to face the truth, the wisdom to act and strength to act on what's revealed. I'll need to embrace the journey for what it is. That'll include the pain, hardship and suffering as well as the good parts.

If I'm going to be serious, I'll have to be prepared to cross bridges. The critical transition from one state of being to another should start from the moment I return home. I'll need to anticipate the bridges from an old me to a new me, what resistance I'll face, what resources I might need to face the transition.

I could not leave Chartres without mentioning my fellow pilgrims. Cheryl, Beth, Jane, MJ and Maureen were keen searchers, too. Beth described our lives as 'an ongoing contemplative journey.' With our different backgrounds and experience, we were seeking answers to similar questions. I admired the mutual respect and preparedness to listen and to understand each other, the sense of wonder at the eye-opening experience that Tim and Jill offered us. We shared the gift of our presence with each other. We found the sacred in the ordinary, in our singing together and our conversation over a good bottle of French wine. It was sad to say goodbye. Another Camino parting!

My deeply personal journey continues.

At one stage I thought my travelling was a reaction to Maris' death but it is more than that, more than working my way through my grieving. The same profound longing that sent me travelling in 2005 and 2006 continues to drive me. It had me walking the Camino in 2010 and 2011. It had me visiting Chartres. I came with many questions, a preparedness to be open and to trust. I hope I have been receptive, and have accepted the challenge to grow with each experience. I leave with a lot more questions than I arrived with. I'm not sure if they will ever be answered or if they are answerable. Perhaps I have to accept that to be human is to live with uncertainty. Perhaps I have to remind myself that a mature spirituality is to bear with the ambiguity of life. Let's hope I have the momentum to nurture this new understanding and not accept certainties just to allay my anxieties. I'll never stop searching and puzzling for answers.

I've heard that your world is supposed to get smaller as you age. It's supposed to close in but, for me, it has the promise of getting vast. My pilgrimage has added meaning to my life and breathed a new vitality into my body and spirit.

I'll just continue to be a pilgrim on a journey and *'walk on, and on, and ever on.'*

ACKNOWLEDGEMENTS

I would like to thank the Universal Music Publishing Group – Australia for the use of 'The Servant Song'.

'THE SERVANT SONG'
Words and music by Richard Gillard
© Universal Music – Brentwood Benson Publishing administered
by Universal Music Publishing MGB Australia Pty Ltd
All rights reserved. International copyright secured.
Reprinted with permission.

I would also like to thank Jill Kimberly Hartwell Geoffrion for permission to use her photograph of the labyrinth at Chartres Cathedral.

The following are guidebooks I found useful.

Alison Raju: *The Way of St James (Pyrenees-Santiago-Finisterre) A Walker's Guide.* Cicerone. 2003.

Alison Raju: *The Way of St James (Le Puy to the Pyrenees) A Walker's Guide.* Cicerone. 2010.

Alison Raju: *Pilgrim Guides to Roads through France to Santiago de Compostela. (Le Puy to the Pyrenees).* Confraternity of Saint Jams. 2006.

William Bisset (ed.): *Pilgrim Guides to Spain (Camino Francés – Saint Jean-Pied-de-Port to Santiago de Compostela).* Confraternity of Saint James. 2007.

François Lepère et Michel Delattre: *Sur le Chemin de Saint-Jacques-de-Compostelle (La via Podiensis, la voie historique...).* Lepère Editions.

François Lepère et Michel Delattre: *Sur le Chemin de Saint-Jacques-de-Compostelle (Le Camino Francés).* Lepère Editions.

Where I have referred to my guidebook, the quotes are from the books by Alison Raju.

The following two are gems. They list every establishment (accommodation, bars, restaurants, supermarkets) along the Camino. Although French, the text is easy to follow because of the extensive use of symbols.

Lauriane Clouteau – Jacques Clouteau: *Miam Miam Dodo. Le Chemin de Saint Jacques de Compostelle (Le Voie du Puy) Les Editions du Vieux Crayon.* 2010.

Marie-Virginie Cambriels – Laurane Clouteau: *Miam Miam Dodo. Le Chemin de Saint Jacques de Compostelle. (El Camino Francés).* Les Editions du Vieux Crayon. 2011

The following two were my spiritual guides:

Gaële de la Brosse (ed.): *Guide Spirituel de Chemins de Saint-Jacques.* Presses de la Renaissance. 2010.

Guide Spirituel du Pèlerin en Chemin avec Saint-Jacques. Communauté des Prémontrés, Abbaye Sainte Foy, Conques. 2008.

I read these accounts as part of my preparation for the Camino.

Kevin A. Codd: *To the Field of Stars. A Pilgrim's Journey to Santiago de Compostela*. William B Erdsmans Publishing Company. 2008.

Conrad Rudolph: *Pilgrimage to the End of the Earth. The Road to Santiago de Compostela*. University of Chicago Press. 2004.

Arthur Paul Boers: *The Way is Made by Walking. A Pilgrimage Along the Camino de Santiago*. IVP Books. 2007.

Tony Kevin: *Walking the Camino. A Modern Pilgrimage to Santiago*. Scribe. 2007.

Jonathan Drane: *The Way of a Thousand Arrows. An Australian Family's Journey through the Camino de Santiago*. Greenshoot. 2007.

Almis Simankevicius: *Santiago. Walking the Pilgrim Path*. Good Walking Books. 2002.

These two were wonderful companions on my visit to Chartres.

Jill Kimberly Hartwell Geoffrion: *Praying the Labyrinth. A Journey for Spiritual Exploration*. The Pilgrim Press. 1999.

Jill Kimberly Hartwell Geoffrion: *Praying the Chartres Labyrinth. A Pilgrim's Guidebook*. The Pilgrim Press. 2006.

This is the story of Noel who lost Maris, his beloved wife of 42 years, to suicide following years of struggling with depression.

The abrupt ending of a life by suicide can be the most catastrophic of events for those left behind. Survivors experience intense pain and massive guilt. Grief banishes survivors to a place so removed from the normal hurly-burly of everyday life that they feel close to madness. Somehow they have to claw their way back.

Noel accepted there was no way around his anguish and met suffering head on. His pain allowed him to discover the richness within him and to grow in wisdom which he hopes might be of benefit to others.

Maris' death did not shut her out of Noel's life. She remains a very real presence. This is a love story with a difference.

'An involving account of the devastation, guilt and pain commonly experienced by people bereaved by suicide. It is a moving love story and a tale of resilience, offering reassurance and a sense of hope to others similarly bereaved.'
–Barbara Hocking, OAM Executive Director, SANE Australia

'Noel Braun gives us the honour of travelling his suicide grief journey after the loss of his beloved wife Maris. He lets us walk with him and understand the devastation that suicide brings and his road of learning to find hope again.'
–Michelle Linn-Gust, Ph D., President-Elect, American Association of Suicidology

'Noel takes us into his innermost thoughts, feelings and emotions as he describes, with incredible love and candour, 'losing' his Maris. Noel's story is immensely powerful and the depth and duration of his grief is testament to his enduring love for Maris.'
–Kate Friis, Counsellor and Psychotherapist

A fter a childhood in the Western Australian surf, Vince Kelly, burning with a desire to save mankind, enters the Catholic priesthood. In contrast, his beach mate, Jamie Griffiths, lacking any direction, drifts into a disastrou job and marriage.

Following his unwitting involvement in Jamie's mother's death, Vince suffer an emotional and spiritual crisis, shattering all his former rock solid beliefs. I desperation, he quits both Perth and the priesthood. He crosses the desert t Sydney and settles in Manly, hoping to find new meaning and purpose.

As soon as he sees the quaint Federation house in Whistler Street, he know it's an ideal refuge for his recovery. He transforms the house into a home, make new friends and begins to rebuild his life but is plagued with indecision and guil

Back in Perth the despairing Jamie cries for help. Already guilt-ridden a abandoning his lifelong mate, Vince leaves Manly, painfully aware that on hi return he must make some vital decisions about his own direction.

'Braun is a deft writer … good storytelling … with a revelation at the end that strengthens the work. A good read.'
—Wendy O'Hanlon, *Acres Australia*